MAJOR MIDDLE EASTERN PROBLEMS IN INTERNATIONAL LAW

Presented by the American Enterprise Institute for Public Policy Research as the eighth study within the framework of its Middle East Research Project, George Lenczowski, director.

AJOR MIDDLE EASTERN PROBLEMS IN INTERNATIONAL LAW

EDITED BY
MAJID KHADDURI

American Enterprise Institute for Public Policy Research
Washington, D.C.

CONTRIBUTORS

JOHN ANTHONY is assistant editor of the *Middle East Journal*.

HERBERT DIXON is assistant professor, American University of Cairo, Egypt.

MAJID KHADDURI, distinguished research professor, School of Advanced International Studies, The Johns Hopkins University, also is president of the Shaybani Society of International Law.

MICHAEL VAN DUSEN is staff consultant to the Committee on Foreign Affairs, House of Representatives, U.S. Congress.

QUINCY WRIGHT was professor emeritus of international law, University of Chicago, and also, in a distinguished career, served as president of the American Society of International Law.

Foreign Affairs Study 3, June 1972
Price $4.00 per copy

© 1972 by American Enterprise Institute for Public Policy Research, Washington, D.C.
Permission to quote from or to reproduce materials in this publication is granted when due acknowledgment is made.
Library of Congress Catalog Card No. L.C. 72-85050

To the students and alumni
of the Middle East Studies program at the
School of Advanced International Studies, The Johns Hopkins University
who in pursuit of a deeper understanding
of Middle Eastern Affairs
have prepared themselves for a better world order

CONTENTS

       LIST OF MAPS

PREFACE

The Middle East is renowned as the birthplace of the oldest legal codes in the world. These codes—Jewish, Christian and Islamic, as well as the ancient Egyptian, Babylonian and Persian—were founded on religion and held to be sanctioned by God. In them, the spirit of the Middle Eastern peoples may be said to be enshrined. Seen as originating from sacred sources, the law held a high place in the eyes of peoples who lived under divine guidance. Small wonder that the ancient sages were viewed as prophets communicating not only God's will and justice but also His divine law. Although this law—at least certain parts of it—has been replaced or superseded by modern legislation, its prestige is still very high in that part of the world and ancient legal traditions continue to provide the basis for judicial decisions.

In modern times the Middle East has been confronted with an influx of foreign ideas and pressures which have undermined ancient legal heritages. Moreover, the conflicts resulting from clash of foreign and domestic interests have often been approached on political rather than legal grounds. As a result, some of the problems that have arisen under the impact of foreign pressures have become too complex to solve by legal methods. In addition, the task of separating the political and legal elements of these problems has become exceedingly difficult.

It is not our purpose in this volume to provide a highly technical and exhaustive treatment of all contemporary Middle Eastern legal problems. Rather, we present here a survey that seeks to elucidate the juridical and diplomatic elements of major problems within the framework of international law and to indicate possibilities for peaceful methods of settlement. This being the case, we do not address problems arising from oil concessions. Further, it should be noted that this volume is designed with the general reader in mind, not the specialist. Finally, the system of transliteration used here is the one followed in the press and not the one to which the editor has conformed in his other published works.

The editor and contributors wish to thank all who helped in the preparation of this volume. In particular, they wish to acknowledge the contribution of the late Professor Quincy Wright who prepared the main part of Chapter 2, on which he was working at the time of his death in October 1970. Professor Wright was the dean of American international lawyers and a true friend of peace in the Middle East throughout a distinguished career that spanned half a century. In addition, a special note of appreciation is due to David Finnie, a member of the New York Bar, who served as a special consultant on this volume and who provided invaluable suggestions. The authors also wish to thank William Sands, George Lenczowski, R. K. Ramazani, who read and commented upon the work in whole or in part, and Marlene McKinley who prepared the index. Any errors that remain uncorrected and the views expressed are, of course, the responsibility of the editor and the contributors.

Majid Khadduri

I. THE EVOLUTION OF MODERN SOVEREIGNTY AND COLLECTIVE SECURITY IN THE MIDDLE EAST

The Islamic State

The whole Middle East was once part of the Islamic empire. Islamic law (the *Shari'a*) was the law of the land, binding on all, Muslims and non-Muslims alike, except in matters of personal status such as marriage, adoption, and inheritance, where each confessional community followed its own canon law. Islamic law, grounded in the Koran, was essentially personal, governing the relationships of individuals and groups among themselves as well as with the outside world.[1] All Muslims were regarded as equal citizens under the rule of one supreme authority, the caliph, and Islamic territory was conceived as one state governed by the law of peace. By contrast, according to Muslim legal doctrine the Islamic state was regarded as being in a permanent state of war with non-Muslim states, and the law of war—the *jihad* (strife)—governed the relationships between Muslim and non-Muslim states. This permanent state of war, however, did not exclude the possibility of conducting diplomatic intercourse or the signing of peace treaties— necessarily of short duration, not exceeding ten years in principle—when the *jihad* was in abeyance.[2]

By the 16th century, however, despite the conceptual unity of the Islamic state, the Muslim world actually consisted of three distinct and relatively stable political entities: the empires of the Ottomans, the Persians, and the Moguls. The division of a doctrinally unified Islam into separate territorial units entailed consideration of legal questions hitherto unknown to Islamic law: How were two or more fully sovereign Islamic entities to coexist? How could territorial frontiers be drawn between them? How could there be established a new mode of loyalty for the citizens on the basis of separate territorial identity, side by side with their common loyalty to Islam? Moreover, this was at the time of the great European expansion, which involved increasing diplomatic and commercial intercourse as new areas were explored and "discovered." Muslim states started adopting some European diplomatic and legal practices to regulate their inter-relationships; sometimes they sought European good offices to resolve disputes between them. For instance, the existence of Persia and Ottoman Turkey as two independent Muslim states necessitated consideration of their separate juristic existence under the broad framework of Islamic unity. As is described in more detail in Chapter IV, Turkey and Persia accepted European intervention in agreeing to establish permanent peace, and in 1847 they signed a treaty recognizing each other's existence (Treaty of

---

[1] See M. Khadduri and H. J. Liebesny, eds., *Law in the Middle East* (Washington, D.C., 1955).

[2] For an exposition of the classical doctrines of Islam governing war and peace, see M. Khadduri, *War and Peace in the Law of Islam* (Baltimore, 1955); M. Hamidullah, *The Muslim Conduct of State,* 3rd ed. (Lahore, 1953).

1

Erzurum);[3] it was not until 1913 that the boundaries between these two states were delimited, and again the good offices of England and Russia were used.[4]

Turkey and Persia were the first two independent Muslim states to emerge, each adhering to a different Islamic creed—Turkey as a Sunni and Persia as a Shi'i country. A third unit, the Mogul empire, whose people upheld the Sunni creed, coalesced in Central Asia and the northern part of the Indian subcontinent. After the fall of the Mogul dynasty in the 18th century, India passed under British control and Central Asia was gradually absorbed by Russia, leaving Afghanistan as an independent Muslim state. All Arab lands in Asia and North Africa, except Morocco, were subjected to Ottoman rule in the sixteenth century. Morocco, a fourth independent Muslim political entity, came under French influence at the opening of the 20th century. Of all of these, only the Ottoman Empire developed a workable system that recognized the identity of the diverse ethnic groups within its territory while maintaining the ecumenical principle of the state. This system vanished with the breakup of the Ottoman Empire after World War I. When the component parts—largely Arab—finally emerged as modern nation-states, they abandoned traditional Islamic doctrine in matters of international law, while some of them, notably Saudi Arabia and Yemen, continued to adhere more or less exclusively to Islamic law as the basis of domestic jurisprudence.

Western vs. Traditional Concepts of International Law

Foreign influence began to encroach seriously on the traditional Islamic lands in the 19th century: Russia came first, entering the Caucasus and Central Asia; then Great Britain established a position in the Persian Gulf, South Arabia and the Nile Valley; and France moved into North Africa. This penetration reached its height after World War I, with British mandates under the League of Nations in Iraq, Palestine, and Transjordan, and French mandates in Syria and Lebanon. After World War II, British and French influence gradually receded, and with the British withdrawal from the Persian Gulf in 1971, the Arab countries were all fully independent states.[5]

These political changes, resulting eventually in the inclusion of all Middle Eastern countries in the modern community of nations, had gradual but profound effects not only on the attitudes of these countries toward non-Muslim countries, but also on their relations with each other. Of crucial importance from the standpoint of international law was acceptance by Muslim governments of the principle that the conduct of foreign relations should be separated from religious doctrine. Perhaps an equally significant corollary was the adoption of the principle of peaceful relations among nations of different religions, which superseded the

---

[3] Text in Sir Edward Hertslet, *Treaties and Other Agreements Concluded Between Great Britain and Persia* (London, 1891), pp. 163-68; J. C. Hurewitz, *Diplomacy in the Near and Middle East* (Princeton, 1956), vol. I, pp. 90-92.

[4] See Sir Arnold Wilson, *South West Persia* (London, 1941), Chapter 10.

[5] For a brief account of British and French colonial ventures in the Middle East, see Harold Nicolson, *Curzon: The Last Phase* (London, 1934); H. W. V. Temperley, *A History of the Peace Conference of Paris* (London, 1924), vol. VI; A. J. Toynbee, *Survey of International Affairs, 1925*, vol. I: *The Islamic World Since the Peace Settlement* (London, 1927).

classical doctrine of the permanent state of war between Muslim and non-Muslim states. In the 20th century the *jihad*, the Islamic law of war, was no longer an adequate basis for Islam's relations with the rest of the world. Also, in accordance with Western legal concepts, the Muslim states for the most part adapted themselves to an international jurisprudence based on territorial sovereignty.[6]

At the same time, however, Islamic law, essentially a personal law, remained as a powerful influence, especially in matters concerning personal status. Muslim institutional patterns did not change simply because these states came to accept Western principles and practices regulating the conduct of external relations. Disputes and misunderstandings were bound to arise when Islamic doctrines came into conflict with those of the West. Sir William Scott, in a decision of the High Court of the Admiralty in 1804, wisely cautioned that Western law should not always be strictly applied to Muslims:

> The inhabitants of those countries [the Ottoman Empire] are not professors of exactly the same law of nations with ourselves; in consideration of the peculiarities of their situation and character, the Court has repeatedly expressed a disposition not to hold them bound to the utmost rigour of that system of public law, on which European states have so long acted, in their intercourse with one another.[7]

Since World War II the Middle Eastern states have actively participated with Western states, in the United Nations and elsewhere, in maintaining international peace and security on the basis of reciprocity and mutual interest. As we shall see, however, their adaptation to Western concepts has not prevented them from voicing objection to practices conducted in the name of international law which seemed to produce results at variance with their own national interests. Modern international law, essentially Western and alien, has sometimes been viewed in its application as inadequate or unjust. Its application to questions of a strictly regional, Islamic character is sometimes seen as supererogatory. Nevertheless, in recent years the Middle Eastern countries, along with other non-Western countries, have displayed an extraordinary interest in the development and codification of international law, and an appreciation of its pervasive influence upon the course of their affairs.

Former Ottoman Territories Gain Their Independence

As noted above, the breakup of the Ottoman Empire following World War I eliminated a major political entity founded on the traditional Islamic system—the universal state. Some of the successor states, like Turkey, Hijaz and Najd (later merged into Saudi Arabia), and Oman became fully independent. Most of them, however, though remodeled along Western constitutional lines, did not immediately acquire full independence in the international legal sense.

At the outset, under the Treaty of Sèvres (1920),[8] Turkey was required to

---

[6] For a discussion of these changes, see M. Khadduri, *The Islamic Law of Nations* (Baltimore, 1966), pp. 60-70.

[7] See the *Madonna del Burso,* High Court of the Admiralty, 1804, 4C. Rob. 169.

[8] Great Britain, *Treaty Series* no. 11 (1920), Cmd. 964; Hurewitz, *Diplomacy,* vol. II, pp. 81-89.

give up a considerable portion of its territory, but under the nationalist movement led by Kemal Atatürk the country fought a war which restored it to full independence. In accordance with the Treaty of Lausanne (1923),[9] Turkey's full sovereignty was respected; by an exchange of population with Greece and Bulgaria all territory inhabited by a majority of Turks became part of the country. The centuries-old practice of giving certain consular and judicial privileges to foreigners, known as the capitulations, was abolished. Passage through the Turkish Straits, long a bone of contention between the Ottoman Porte and the powers, was regulated by a special convention, but Turkey's full sovereignty was recognized.[10]

When Turkey entered into membership of the League of Nations in 1937 and became a founding member of the United Nations in 1945, it had already given up sovereignty over all its former Arab territories. Earlier Turkey had claimed that Mosul and Alexandretta, whose inhabitants consisted of Arabs, Turks, and Kurds, should be restored to it. The settlement of these disputes, in which the League of Nations had played a significant role, resulted in the annexation of Mosul by Iraq (1926) and the return of Alexandretta to Turkey (1939).[11]

When Turkey gave up its control over Arab lands to the "parties concerned" (Treaty of Lausanne)[12]—a clause interpreted to mean that Turkey relinquished its sovereignty in favor of the inhabitants of the territory—the Allied Powers had agreed that the independence of the former Ottoman provinces, in accordance with the terms of the League of Nations mandates, was to be "provisionally recognized."[13] The Hijaz, Najd, Yemen and Oman became fully independent; but sovereignty over the peripheries of Arabia—Kuwait, Bahrain, Qatar, Aden and the Hadhramaut—had already been qualified by treaty arrangements. Turkey's surrender of its nominal sovereignty over these territories was interpreted to mean surrender to the party in control of these territories—Great Britain.[14]

Iraq, Syria, Lebanon, Palestine, and Transjordan (later Jordan)—collectively called the Fertile Crescent—though inherently sovereign, were considered not yet able to stand alone. They were therefore placed under the temporary tutelage of Britain and France until they would become independent, according to the terms of the mandates. Mandatory control was administered under the supervision of the League of Nations, but neither the league nor the Mandatory Powers possessed

---

[9] Great Britain, *Treaty Series* no. 16 (1923), Cmd. 1929; Hurewitz, *Diplomacy*, vol. II, pp. 119-27.

[10] See Chapter IV, below.

[11] For a discussion of the Mosul dispute, see Q. Wright, "The Mosul Dispute," *American Journal of International Law*, vol. 20 (1926) pp. 453 ff.; M. Khadduri, "The Alexandretta Dispute," ibid., vol. 39 (1945), pp. 406-25.

[12] Article 16, The Treaty of Lausanne.

[13] Article 22 of the League of Nations Covenant.

[14] For an interesting legal analysis, see Issam Abdel Rahman Azzam, "The International Status of the Persian Gulf States: Kuwait, Bahrain, Qatar," *Revue Egyptien de Droit International*, no. 15 (1959). For the treaties between Great Britain and South Arabia and the Persian Gulf States, see the relevant texts in Hurewitz, *Diplomacy*, vol. I.

sovereignty over the mandated territories; they merely exercised it on behalf of the peoples of the mandated territories until they became fully independent.[15]

The first country to be emancipated from the mandate was Iraq. In a 1930 treaty, Great Britain promised to defend Iraq in case of foreign attack and to consult with her on foreign policy. Britain obtained two air bases from Iraq as well as the use of internal communications in case Britain was involved in war with another power. Britain also promised to recommend to the League of Nations termination of the mandate and granting the country independence.[16] In 1932 the mandate came to an end and Iraq attained full international status when she was admitted to membership in the league.[17] The Anglo-Iraqi treaty, invoked during World War II presumably for the defense of Iraq, was terminated and replaced by an agreement giving Iraq control over the air bases in 1955, when Iraq signed the Baghdad Pact with Britain and Turkey.[18] In 1958, after a military revolution, Iraq decided to withdraw from the Baghdad Pact (later renamed CENTO).[19]

While Syria and Lebanon were promised independence as Iraq was, the French mandate continued until World War II. In 1941, the Free French in cooperation with British forces entered Syria and Lebanon and declared the independence of these two countries. Two years later, in 1943, national governments were established following general elections. Legal problems arose, however, in connection with the declaration of independence before the termination of the mandate, because the League of Nations was not in session and only its Council had power to terminate the mandate.[20] The powers, however, had extended recognition to Syria and Lebanon and both were represented at the San Francisco conference in 1945 to participate in the drafting of the Charter of the United Nations as founding members. In its final meeting in 1946, the Council of the League of Nations decided to terminate the mandate over Syria and Lebanon. Presumably this applied retroactively, terminating the mandate status before independence was recognized.[21]

In 1946 Britain declared her intention to recognize the independence of Transjordan. The Transjordanian mandate, like those of Syria and Lebanon, had been terminated by the League of Nations after independence was granted. The internal constitutional structure was modified to prepare Transjordan for this step:

---

[15] For a discussion of the theory and practice of the mandates system see Quincy Wright, *Mandates Under the League of Nations* (Chicago, 1930), Chapter 10.

[16] Text of the treaty in Great Britain, *Treaty Series* no. 15 (1930), Cmd. 3797; Hurewitz, *Diplomacy,* vol. II, pp. 178-81.

[17] For a discussion of the termination of the Iraq mandate and the achievement of independence, see M. Khadduri, *Independent Iraq,* 2nd ed. (London, 1960), pp. 309-17.

[18] Great Britain, *Treaty Series* no. 50 (1955), Cmd. 9544; Hurewitz, *Diplomacy,* vol. II, pp. 391-95.

[19] For a discussion of the Baghdad Pact and its denunciation, see Waldemar Gallman, *Iraq Under General Nuri* (Baltimore, 1962); and M. Khadduri, *Republican Iraq* (London, 1969), pp. 184-85.

[20] For a discussion of this problem, see M. Khadduri, "The Franco-Lebanese Dispute and the Crisis of November 1943," *American Journal of International Law,* vol. 38 (1944), pp. 601-20.

[21] For the working of the French mandate in Syria and Lebanon, see S. H. Longrigg, *Syria and Lebanon Under French Mandate* (London, 1958).

Amir Abdullah, ruler of the country, was proclaimed King and a cabinet responsible to parliament was appointed. A treaty between Great Britain and Transjordan, regulating the relationships between the two countries on the basis of independence and continuing British assurance of military and economic assistance, was signed in 1948.[22] This treaty was later revised to recognize changes in the status of Transjordan, notably its transformation into Jordan after the incorporation of Arab Palestine in 1950. The pact was finally terminated in 1956, although the traditional friendship between Jordan and Britain continued. Jordan became a member of the United Nations in 1955.[23]

This section has described how most of the mandated territories of the Middle East ultimately achieved national independence. Only Palestine remains to be considered—and because Palestine is a very special case, discussion will be deferred to the next chapter.

The Independence of Egypt and Sudan

Since League of Nations mandates were not involved, Egypt and the Sudan fall into a different category as successor states. Emerging as a self-governing province early in the 19th century, Egypt passed through various stages of development until its independence was declared in 1922. From the time of the appointment of Muhammad Ali as governor in 1805, Egypt began to attain the status of a suzerainty and to rise into a fully self-governing country within the Ottoman Empire. In 1863, the Khedive, ruler of Egypt, was granted by the Ottoman sultan limited powers to enter into contractual agreements with foreign powers, subject to the approval of the sultan. Egypt thereby received the right to establish a separate army as well as a separate judicial system. These powers, modified slightly in 1879, especially concerning the reduction of the army, remained essentially unchanged in theory until World War I. Even though Egypt passed under British occupation in 1882, following a military revolt in 1880 which threatened foreign interests, it remained in law part of the Ottoman Empire and continued to pay annual tribute.[24]

In 1914, Egypt was declared to be a protectorate under Britain. All powers of defense and foreign relations passed to Britain when the Ottoman Empire entered the war on the side of the Central Powers. The protectorate lasted until 1922, when Egypt was declared independent, subject to four reserved points which were to be the basis of subsequent negotiation between Britain and Egypt: the defense of Egypt against attack, the protection of imperial communications (Suez Canal), the protection of minorities, and the Sudan. In the interim, Turkey, under the Treaty of Lausanne, had relinquished its sovereignty over Egypt and the Sudan, as in other Arab countries, to the "parties concerned." Since Egypt's independence

---

[22] Great Britain, *Treaty Series* no. 26 (1948), Cmd. 7404; Hurewitz, *Diplomacy,* vol. II, pp. 296-99.

[23] For Anglo-Jordanian relations, see King Hussein, *Uneasy Lies the Head* (London, 1962); Lt. General Sir John B. Glubb, *A Soldier with the Arabs* (London, 1957).

[24] For a study of the legal status of Egypt under the Ottoman Empire, see Vernon A. O'Rourke, *The Juristic Status of Egypt and the Sudan* (Baltimore, 1935).

had already been declared, Turkey's renunciation of its sovereignty over Egypt in 1923 was obviously in favor of the Egyptian people.

Not until 1936 did Britain and Egypt come to an agreement on the four "reserved points." In the Anglo-Egyptian treaty of that year, Britain relinquished not only its claim to the protection of minorities, but also the right to defend British imperial communications in Egypt other than those related to the maintenance of the British base in the Canal Zone. The question of the Sudan, however, was left for future negotiation. Britain and Egypt agreed in the treaty to consult each other specifically on foreign affairs and on any other matter in which they had common interests. Britain promised, for example, to defend Egypt in case of foreign attack; Egypt, in exchange, granted Britain the right to use her internal means of communication during any war in which Egypt might be involved.[25] It was also agreed that the Mixed Courts were to be abolished, subject to the approval of the powers signatories to the convention relating to the Mixed Courts.[26] In 1937 a convention was signed by Egypt and the powers (at Montreux), providing for the termination of the Mixed Courts regime within 12 years from the time of the coming into force of the convention; in 1949, therefore, Egypt's jurisdiction over its judicial system became complete.[27] In 1937 Egypt also became a member of the League of Nations and thereby attained full international status. There remained the lingering questions of the Suez base, the closure of the Suez Canal to nonsignatory powers, and other questions that arose after World War II.

Before the 19th century, the Sudan was not part of the Ottoman Empire. In 1821 Muhammad Ali, governor of Egypt, occupied the Sudan with Egyptian forces. It became, *ipso jure,* part of Ottoman sovereignty since Muhammad Ali derived his powers of action from the sultan. The country remained under Egyptian control until 1880, when a native revolt, under the religious leadership of the Mahdi, expelled the Ottoman-Egyptian administration.[28] Reconquest of the Sudan was carried out in 1897 under British command and a joint British-Egyptian control, called the Condominium, was established in 1898.[29] This situation continued until 1956 when the Sudan, upon British withdrawal, was given the choice between independence and unity with Egypt. The Sudan decided to become independent, and its rise to full international status was recognized by Britain, Egypt, and other powers.[30]

---

25 Text of the treaty in Great Britain, *Treaty Series* no. 6 (1936), Cmd. 5360; Hurewitz, *Diplomacy,* vol. II, pp. 203-11. For a discussion of the treaty, see M. Y. Zayid, *Egypt's Struggle for Independence* (Beirut, 1965).

26 The jurisdiction of the Mixed Courts, composed of jurists of several nationalities, extended to all suits "between Egyptians and foreigners and between foreigners of different nationalities," as well as disputes between all foreigners involving land.

27 J. Y. Brinton, *The Mixed Courts of Egypt,* 2nd ed. (New Haven, 1968); William Tracy, "Jasper Yates Brinton: An American Judge in Egypt" and "The Mixed Courts of Egypt," *Aramco World Magazine,* vol. 21, no. 5 (September-October 1970), pp. 18-21.

28 A. B. Theobold, *The Mahdiya* (London, 1951).

29 For a discussion of the legal status of the Sudan, see O'Rourke, *Juristic Status,* and M. Shibeika, *British Policy in the Sudan, 1882-1902* (London, 1952).

30 Makki Shibeika, *Independent Sudan* (New York, 1959); K. D. D. Henderson, *Sudan Republic* (New York, 1965).

Regional Security Pacts

The idea that Middle Eastern countries should cooperate among themselves after independence to maintain regional peace and security has its origins in the period prior to World War II. A limited version of the idea first took root in the Balkans of which Turkey formed a part. Subsequently the idea was extended, at the initiative of Turkey, to encompass a treaty relationship among Turkey, Iran and Iraq, known as the Saadabad Pact. This treaty, now only of historical significance, provides a background for understanding the subsequent evolution of the Baghdad Pact and CENTO.

In the mid-thirties, when Mussolini's Italy took on the appearance of an aggressive Mediterranean power following its successful occupation of Ethiopia (Libya having already come under Italian control in 1911), Turkey was among those countries anxious to discuss the problem of regional security in the Middle East. Iran (Persia) and Iraq were both approached but the initial negotiations were confined to Turkey and Persia. A draft pact was initiated between these countries in 1935 without Iraq's participation, since Iraq and Persia were then engaged in a disagreement over the passage through the River Shatt al-Arab. Turkey offered its good offices in 1936, and the Shatt question, withdrawn from the League of Nations, was settled by direct negotiation in Teheran in 1937.[31] With this dispute out of the way (for the time being), representatives of Turkey and Afghanistan joined Iraq and Iran in signing a four-power Middle Eastern pact at the Shah's Saadabad Palace on the outskirts of Teheran on July 8, 1937. The Saadabad Pact provided for consultation among the four powers in all disputes concerning their common interests (Article 3); the inviolability of their common frontiers (Article 2); and the noninterference in the domestic affairs of each other's country (Articles 1, 7). Article 4 stipulated that the four powers should not "resort, whether singly or jointly with one or more third Powers, to any act of aggression directed against any other of the Contracting Parties." It was also agreed to bring any violation of Article 4 to the Council of the League of Nations (Article 5). An act of aggression by one of the contracting parties would entitle the others to denounce the pact with respect to the party in question (Article 6).[32] In a separate protocol, signed on the same day, the four powers agreed to set up a permanent council, which was to meet at least once a year, with an attached secretariat. However, the council met only once, while the representatives of the four powers were still in Teheran. Thus the Saadabad Pact, like many other regional pacts among smaller powers, meant little more than a pious declaration of goodwill on the part of the signatories; in practice, it failed to provide either solidarity among the members or the security they desired from outside attack. The Saadabad Pact became virtually a dead letter when World War II broke out, and it was never revived.

---

[31] See Chapter IV, below.

[32] Text in Hurewitz, *Diplomacy*, vol. II, pp. 214-16; League of Nations, *Treaty Series*, vol. 190 (1938), pp. 21-27. The pact was to be in force for five years in the first instance, and deemed to be renewed for successive five-year periods in the absence of denunciation.

The Baghdad Pact and CENTO

The initiative to encourage the Middle Eastern countries to cooperate among themselves for the maintenance of peace and security was taken by the United States. America's interest in the defense of the region following World War II was first demonstrated in the Truman Doctrine of 1947 and later in its participation in attempts to solve the Palestine question and the Arab-Israeli disputes. The United States urged Great Britain to come to an understanding with Egypt, and this urging contributed to the Anglo-Egyptian agreement of 1954, under which Britain evacuated its Suez Canal base. Egypt itself did not wish to take part in organizing a regional security system, fearing that such an arrangement might result in the renewal of an alliance with Britain. But Britain and the United States considered the Middle East an important strategic region for defense against Soviet expansion, and they sought to enlist the cooperation of other Middle Eastern countries. Turkey and Greece both joined the North Atlantic Treaty Organization (NATO), and the United States endeavored to extend to the Middle East a defense system in which Middle East states could help to contain the threat of expansion by the Soviet Union.

Turkey took the initiative in developing a security structure involving the Middle East. Its attempts to enlist the cooperation of Egypt failed, but negotiations with Iraq, with which Turkey had already entered into an agreement in 1946, were successful. The Turko-Iraqi pact, later called the Baghdad Pact, was signed on February 24, 1955. It was the first link in the "northern tier" defense system, later joined by Great Britain, Pakistan and Iran.

The pact provided *inter alia* for mutual cooperation among the signatories for security and defense in accordance with Article 51 [33] of the United Nations Charter (Article 1). The members agreed that after the pact came into force they would determine the measures to be taken, which would become operative after approval by their respective governments (Article 2). They also agreed to refrain from interference in each other's internal affairs and to settle disputes among themselves peacefully in accordance with the United Nations Charter (Article 3). A permanent council, assisted by a secretariat and a number of committees, was provided to manage the defense system.[34]

Other Arab countries were invited to adhere to the Baghdad Pact in accordance with Article 5, but they refused. Egypt began to attack the pact on the ground that it violated the Arab security pact, even though Article 4 declared that nothing in it would derogate from the international obligations of the signatories with regard to any third state or states. Inter-Arab rivalry at this time became nonetheless so

---

[33] Article 51 of the United Nations Charter states: "Nothing in the present Charter shall impair the inherent right of individual or collective self-defense if an armed attack occurs against a Member of the United Nations, until the Security Council has taken measures necessary to maintain international peace and security. Measures taken by Members in the exercise of this right of self-defense shall be immediately reported to the Security Council and shall not in any way affect the authority and responsibility of the Security Council under the present Charter to take at any time such action as it deems necessary in order to maintain or restore international peace and security."

[34] Text of the pact in Great Britain, *Treaty Series*, Misc. 5 (1955), Cmd. 9429; Hurewitz, *Diplomacy*, vol. II, pp. 390-91.

intense that Iraq, after the overthrow of its monarchy in 1958, found it politic to withdraw from the pact in the name of Arab solidarity. The headquarters of the secretariat was then transferred from Baghdad to Ankara, Turkey, and the name was changed to the Central Treaty Organization (CENTO). The United States has never officially joined CENTO, but has participated in the work of its various committees.

In an attempt to strengthen the CENTO defense system, the United States in 1959 entered into bilateral defense agreements with Turkey, Iran, and Pakistan.[35] Like its forerunner, the Saadabad Pact, however, CENTO as a defense system proved to be of doubtful significance. As a medium of cooperation among its members in other fields, especially economic, it has achieved greater success. Soviet military and other assistance to certain Arab countries, dating from the early mid-1950s in the case of Syria and Egypt, and expanded in these and in other Arab states following the June War of 1967, has further weakened the political and military significance of the pact; in a real sense, CENTO has been outflanked by Soviet penetration into Arab lands.[36]

The Arab League

The idea of forming an organization which would coordinate the activities of Arab states stemmed from Arab national aspirations to unite and create one Arab state, federal or unitary, and not merely to cooperate for regional defense and security. However, when the circumstances for forming a union became favorable during World War II, especially after Britain's decision to support Arab aspirations for unity,[37] the Arab states were reluctant to promote unity. Instead, they met in 1944 in Alexandria and drew up a plan which was more in the nature of a confederation than a federal union. In 1945 the Arab representatives convened in Cairo to sign the pact of an Arab League, stressing the sovereign attributes of the individual members more than cementing the structure laid down at Alexandria the year before.[38] The pact provided for the establishment of an organization whose members were the Arab states which signed the pact and those who desired to adhere to it later. The Arab League was made up of a Council, composed of the representatives of its members, with one vote for every member-state regardless of the number of representatives, a General Secretariat for organizing the work of the league, and a number of committees dealing with social, economic, cultural, and other matters connected with the organization.

The purpose of the league, as stated in its pact, was to promote the common interests of the members, to realize closer collaboration among them, and to safeguard their independence and sovereignty. Since some of the Arab countries had not yet achieved independence and therefore were not eligible for membership, the league extended its scope of interest "to consider in a general way the

---

[35] For an account of the Baghdad Pact, see Gallman, *Iraq Under General Nuri.*

[36] For regional cooperation in the non-Arab countries, see R. K. Ramazani, *The Northern Tier* (Princeton, 1966).

[37] See Anthony Eden's speech in London in 1941 (*The Times,* May 30, 1941), and his statement in Parliament in February 1943.

[38] Text in Hurewitz, *Diplomacy,* vol. II, pp. 245-49.

affairs and interests of the Arab countries" (Article 2). As stated in the pact, cooperation among members was to be provided in the following activities: (1) economic and financial matters, such as trade, customs, currency, industry, et cetera, (2) communications, including railways, roads, aviation, navigation and posts and telegraphs, (3) cultural affairs, (4) nationality, including passports, visas, extradition, et cetera, (5) social welfare, and (6) health matters.

The Arab League, contrary to Arab national aspirations, failed to form a permanent union, federal or otherwise, since the members reserved sovereign rights under which they could withdraw at any moment. It became no more than a confederation, since its members preserved their right to independent action. No decision was binding on any one member unless accepted by that member or carried by a unanimous vote. Nevertheless, the league pledged to coordinate the activities of its members and to settle disputes among its members.

The use of force for the settlement of disputes among members was prohibited. "Should there arise among them a dispute that does not involve the independence of a state, its sovereignty or its territorial integrity, and should the two contending parties apply to the Council for the settlement of this dispute, the decision of the Council shall then be effective and obligatory" (Article 5). The Council would mediate in a dispute which might lead to war between two members or between a member and another state (or states) in order to conciliate them. Decisions relating to arbitration and mediation were to be taken by majority vote only.

In case of aggression or the threat of aggression, the members would request an immediate meeting of the Arab League Council, which would decide, by unanimous vote, upon the measures to be taken against the aggressor. If the aggressor were a member of the Arab League, "the vote of the state will not be counted in determining unanimity" (Article 6). There was no mention of whether sanctions against the aggressor were to be military or economic. Indeed, the only specific sanction to be applied almost automatically was dismissal (Article 18). Withdrawal from the league was otherwise voluntary and might take effect a year following notification to the Council. But if a member did not approve an amendment to the pact carried by two-thirds of the members, that state could withdraw when the amendment became effective.[39]

From the time of its establishment the Arab League has been confronted with serious problems. Several of these occurred before the organization had time to grow and gain in strength. The Franco-Syrian dispute, which arose only a month after the league came into operation, resulted in the calling of an emergency session of the Council in June 1945. The Council served notice in a resolution that the league would take the necessary measures to resist French aggression. Hardly had the Syrian crisis passed when the league was faced with the Palestine problem. Failure to resolve this problem, one of the Arab League's primary concerns, exposed the league's weakness when it failed to muster sufficient strength to forestall the establishment of Israel. This failure may be regarded as the initial cause of Arab lack of confidence in the league to establish solidarity

---

[39] For study of the structure and legal nature of the Arab League, see M. Khadduri, "The Arab League as a Regional Organization," *American Journal of International Law,* vol. 40 (1946), pp. 756-77.

among the Arab states, although it did its utmost to coordinate their activities in the face of reluctance of most members to cooperate on the regional level.

In 1950, following the disastrous Palestine war (see Chapter II), a joint defense and economic cooperation treaty was concluded by Arab League members to coordinate the military power of Arab countries. In accordance with Article 51 of the United Nations Charter and Articles 2 and 6 of the Arab League Pact, the members of the Arab League pledged to maintain peace and security in the region as well as to coordinate their military power for defense against aggression (Articles 3 and 4). "The contracting states consider any armed aggression made against one or more of them or their armed forces, to be directed against them all" (Article 2). A permanent military commission, composed of the general staffs of the Arab states, was formed to draw up joint defense plans and to charge the states with implementation (Article 5). An economic council was also formed to draw plans which would help to achieve the purposes of the joint defense arrangement (Article 8).[40]

The social, economic and cultural plans which the Arab League laid down, if they could be carried out, would have more far-reaching significance in achieving Arab solidarity than its political or military activities. Special committees were organized to study plans of postal and custom unions, unification of communications, expansion of commercial relations, adoption of a single passport system, and cooperation in legal, education, and health matters. Some of these plans were made into legal agreements, but mainly because of political and personal complications within the league it was difficult to put them into effect. Critics condemned the Arab League as a failure because it could not solve pending issues. Others, while conceding defects in its structure and organization, felt that it represented a certain stage of development in Arab regional organization that could form the basis for further improvement.[41] The league, as the secretary general once said, could not rise far above present conditions in inter-Arab relations. If the Arab League is ever dissolved, which is possible, it is likely to be replaced by another organization which gives stronger expression to the desire and need for cooperation in inter-Arab relations and the aspiration for unity which persists among the Arabs.

---

[40] Text in Hurewitz, *Diplomacy,* vol. II, pp. 311-14.

[41] For a study of the Arab League as a regional organization, see R. W. Macdonald, *The Arab League* (Princeton, 1965).

II. THE PALESTINE CONFLICT IN INTERNATIONAL LAW

Historical Background

The previous chapter dealt with the process whereby most of the former Ottoman territories subject to League of Nations mandates between the two world wars ultimately achieved full independence after World War II. Only in respect to Palestine did seemingly insuperable difficulties arise. The status of Palestine was complicated by conflicting commitments on the part of Great Britain during World War I. In the so-called Hussein-McMahon correspondence of 1915-16, Britain promised that after the Ottomans were defeated Palestine would form part of an Arab state or confederation of states.[1] But in the Balfour Declaration of 1917 Britain also promised Zionist leaders the establishment of a Jewish National Home in Palestine.[2] Thus Britain undertook to protect and support the conflicting nationalistic aspirations of Arabs and Jews, hoping that the two might ultimately be reconciled.

When the mandate covering Palestine went into force in 1922, spokesmen for the Arab population of some 800,000 objected to the way it appeared to implement the Balfour Declaration, which they considered inconsistent with the Hussein-McMahon commitments. The Arabs were reassured however, by the issuance of the Churchill white paper of 1922,[3] which interpreted the declaration to mean not an independent Jewish state of Palestine, but a national home in Palestine assuring the Jews the opportunity to immigrate, to develop settlements, and to have access to their religious shrines in the Holy Land on the same basis as Muslims and Christians. Although some Zionists continued to anticipate the eventual establishment of a Jewish state, the Churchill interpretation was accepted by their most prominent leaders, including Chaim Weizmann, president of the World Zionist Organization, Judah Magnes, president of the Hebrew University in Palestine, and leaders of the religious groups that settled in Palestine with the aid of Western European Jewish communities.[4]

---

[1] *Correspondence Between Sir Henry McMahon and the Sherif of Mecca*, Misc. no. 3 (1939), Cmd. 5957; J. C. Hurewitz, *Diplomacy in the Near and Middle East*, vol. II (Princeton, 1956), pp. 13-17; see also Ralph H. Magnus, ed., *Documents on the Middle East* (Washington, D.C.: American Enterprise Institute for Public Policy Research, 1969), pp. 12-26.

[2] Text in Hurewitz, *Diplomacy*, vol. II; see also Leonard Stein, *The Balfour Declaration* (London, 1961); and Magnus, *Documents on the Middle East*, p. 27.

[3] Text in Walter Laqueur, ed., *The Israeli-Arab Reader* (New York: Bantam, 1970), pp. 45-50.

[4] See Quincy Wright, "The Palestine Problem," *Political Science Quarterly*, vol. 41 (1926), pp. 384-412; Wright, "The Middle East Crisis," in *The Middle East: Prospects for Peace* (Dobbs Ferry, N.Y., 1969), pp. 1-40, at p. 16.

During the 1920s comparative peace reigned in Palestine. The British believed that the mandate would continue indefinitely, assuring protection to the three main religious groups—Jews, Muslims and Christians. The Arabs, however, anticipated that Palestine would eventually become an independent Arab state, as seemed to have been promised by the provisions of the mandate requiring the development of "self-governing institutions" (Article 2) and of the League of Nations Covenant provisionally recognizing the independence of the class A mandates (Article 22).[5]

British and Arab anticipations were both shattered by the increase in Jewish immigration, especially following Hitler's persecution of the Jews in the 1930s, by the heightened anxiety of Palestine Arabs as Jewish immigration and land acquisition continued, and by stepped-up pressure from Zionists both in and outside Palestine for a Jewish state.

Several attempts were made to settle the issue before World War II, most notably a partition plan which would have divided Palestine into Arab and Jewish states and created a separate status for Jerusalem. This plan, however, was rejected by the Arabs in 1937.[6] In 1938 a plan for certain local and municipal autonomy was brought out;[7] and in 1939 the British issued a white paper limiting Jewish immigration, preparing the country for self-government and declaring that the Jewish national home had been achieved.[8] This plan, rejected by Zionist leaders,[9] came nearest to satisfying Arab demands; but World War II resulted first in the delay of its implementation and then in its replacement by new plans more favorable to Jewish national aspirations.

The problem reached crisis proportions shortly after the war ended in 1945. Unable to continue to deal with the situation, Britain relinquished to the United Nations its authority as mandatory power. In accord with the majority report of a special committee,[10] the General Assembly approved a resolution on November 29, 1947, for the partition of Palestine into Jewish and Arab states within defined boundaries, internationalization of Jerusalem and surrounding territory containing most of the holy places of three religions, and close economic ties among the three parts of Palestine.[11] Zionists supported the resolution. It was opposed by the Arabs, who maintained that it violated the Charter of the United Nations. During the debate in the General Assembly the Arabs failed by one vote to procure a request to the International Court of Justice for an advisory opinion on Article 80 of the Charter which, they alleged, required consent of the "peoples" of Palestine

---

[5] Text of Palestine mandate in Laqueur, *The Israeli-Arab Reader*, pp. 34-42.

[6] Palestine Royal Commission Report (London, 1937), Cmd. 5479; partial text in Laqueur, *The Israeli-Arab Reader*, pp. 56-58. Known as the Report of the Peel Commission.

[7] *The Palestine Partition Report* (London, 1938), Cmd. 5854.

[8] *Palestine: Statement of Policy* (London, 1939), Cmd. 6019.

[9] See Statement by the Jewish Agency for Palestine, reproduced in Laqueur, *The Israeli-Arab Reader*, pp. 76-77.

[10] Text in Laqueur, *The Israeli-Arab Reader*, pp. 108-12.

[11] Text in Hurewitz, *Diplomacy*, vol. II, pp. 281-95; partial text in Laqueur, *The Israeli-Arab Reader*, pp. 113-22, and Magnus, *Documents on the Middle East*, pp. 144-60. An excellent survey of the background of the Partition Plan is J. C. Hurewitz, *The Struggle for Palestine* (New York, 1950). See also Fanny Andrews, *The Holy Land Under the Mandate* (New York, 1930), 2 vols.; J. M. N. Jeffries, *Palestine: The Reality* (London, 1939); M. F. Abcarius, *Palestine Through the Fog of Propaganda* (London, 1946).

JORDAN VALLEY

for any change in the status of the mandated territory.[12] The Arabs prepared to resist implementation of the resolution.

Hostilities broke out in the winter of 1947-48. Britain declared that it would relinquish all responsibility by the following May 15. The day before this deadline, on May 14, 1948, Israel declared its independence,[13] and was promptly recognized by the United States, the Soviet Union, and many other nations. Hostilities intensified. Brief truces were arranged by Count Bernadotte, the United Nations mediator, who also suggested some changes in the boundaries set out in the United Nations resolution, mostly favorable to the Arabs. (Bernadotte was assassinated in September 1948 by Jewish terrorists.) In the course of the continued hostilities, and largely because of them, more than half a million Arabs fled the country. Early in 1949 a conference of the United Nations Conciliation Commission was held at Lausanne, attended by representatives of the United States, France and Turkey. The commission persuaded Israel and its Arab neighbors, on May 12, 1949, to agree to negotiate boundaries on the basis of the General Assembly resolution of 1947. Israel, however, after occupying more territory, rejected the agreement. Israel was admitted to the United Nations on May 11, 1949. Through the new United Nations mediator, Ralph Bunche, armistice agreements were signed between Israel and each of its Arab neighbors, the last with Syria on July 20, 1949. All the armistice agreements provided for cease-fire on substantially the existing lines of occupation, thus permitting Israel to occupy about 50 percent more territory than it would have been accorded if the United Nations resolution of 1947 had been implemented.[14]

While the Arabs did not accept the 1949 armistice lines as permanent boundaries, Israel functioned within them as a sovereign state and a member of the United Nations. The Arabs, refusing to recognize Israel, instituted a comprehensive economic boycott. To establish effective commercial relations with Asian and African countries, Israel needed free navigation of the Suez Canal and the Gulf of Aqaba. The Arab states closed these waterways to Israeli shipping on the ground that Israel was still in a state of war with them.

In addition, the Arab-Israeli war of 1948-49 had produced several hundred thousand homeless Arab refugees, wards of the United Nations living mostly in makeshift camps just outside Israel's borders, where many of them could witness the taking over of their former lands by Jewish settlers. The refugees were given reason to hope for return to their homes or compensation for property they had lost. Repeated United Nations resolutions calling upon Israel to provide for repatriation or compensation went unheeded. The refugee camps on Israel's borders increasingly became a source of unrest and agitation. As time went on leaders among the refugees began to ask for weapons and other support from

---

[12] "Except as may be agreed upon in individual trusteeship agreements, made under Articles 77, 79, and 81, placing each territory under the trusteeship system, and until such agreements have been concluded, nothing in this Chapter shall be construed in or of itself to alter in any manner the rights whatsoever of any states or any peoples or the terms of existing international instruments to which Members of the United Nations may respectively be parties." (Article 80, section 1.)

[13] Text of Proclamation of Independence in Laqueur, *The Israeli-Arab Reader*, pp. 125-28.

[14] Text of Egyptian-Israeli armistice agreement in Hurewitz, *Diplomacy*, vol. II, pp. 299-304.

Arab governments. Because of popular feelings that had been aroused it was politically difficult for any Arab government to resist such demands. Commandos ("fedayeen") launched incursions into Israeli territory, heightening the tension and often provoking Israel to retaliate in force. Both sides appealed repeatedly to the United Nations, but no settlement was reached despite resolution after resolution condemning violent or illegal acts attributed to one side or the other.

Failure to solve the refugee problem was perhaps the key factor preventing improvement in Arab-Israeli relations. An aroused public opinion put increasing pressure on Arab heads of government, whose rhetorical public statements were often construed in Israel as threats to its peace and security. Militants among the refugees, impatient with inaction, continued raids into Israeli territory. The main commando centers in 1956 were in Egyptian Sinai; Israel regarded Egypt as responsible for the raids and eventually decided to stop the infiltrations by force. On October 29, 1956, Israel invaded Sinai, including Sharm el-Sheikh commanding the Straits of Tiran. Almost simultaneously Britain and France invaded the Suez area, acting largely as a consequence of failure to reach agreement with Egypt over its nationalization of the Suez Canal Company on July 26, 1956. United Nations action, supported by the United States and the Soviet Union, resulted in withdrawal of the invading forces. The 1949 armistice lines were restored; the Straits of Tiran and the Gulf of Aqaba were opened to Israeli shipping; and a United Nations Emergency Force was established on the armistice line in Egyptian territory. Israel refused to allow a United Nations force on its territory, and Egypt permitted the force to remain on its territory only at Egypt's sufferance.

This unstable and unsatisfactory situation, with occasional border raids and retaliations, persisted until the six-day war of June 1967. The June war erupted when Israel launched major air and land attacks against Egypt and Syria in response to measures which Israel considered highly provocative: withdrawal by Egypt of its consent to the presence of the United Nations force on its territory; Egypt's announcement of resumption of the blockade of Israeli shipping in the Gulf of Aqaba; the subsequent movement of Egyptian forces into Sinai; and threatening statements by Syrian and Egyptian leaders indicating intent to destroy Israel.

The June war resulted in Israel's occupation of old Jerusalem and territory west of the Jordan River, the Gaza strip, the Sinai peninsula, and Syria's Golan Heights. Unanimous United Nations resolutions calling for cease-fire on existing lines of occupation were adopted on June 6, 7 and 9, and the cease-fire was eventually accepted by Israel, its Arab neighbors, and by Iraq.

However, peace remained as remote as ever. The refugee problem became even more complex, as many thousands more Palestinians fled the occupied West Bank, mainly to Jordan. On November 22, 1967, the Security Council of the United Nations unanimously adopted its famous Resolution 242, which had been hammered out word by word in extensive negotiations in an effort to provide a basis for settlement. Here is the text of the resolution:

The Security Council

Expressing its continuing concern with the grave situation in the Middle East,

Emphasizing the inadmissibility of the acquisition of territory by war and the need to work for a just and lasting peace in which every State in the area can live in security,

Emphasizing further that all Member States in their acceptance of the Charter of the United Nations have undertaken a commitment to act in accordance with Article 2 of the Charter,

1. *Affirms* that the fulfillment of Charter principles requires the establishment of a just and lasting peace in the Middle East which should include the application of both the following principles:

(i) Withdrawal of Israeli armed forces from territories occupied in the recent conflict;

(ii) Termination of all claims or states of belligerency and respect for and acknowledgement of the sovereignty, territorial integrity and political independence of every State in the area and their right to live in peace within secure and recognized boundaries free from threats or acts of force;

2. *Affirms further* the necessity

(a) For guaranteeing freedom of navigation through international waterways in the area;

(b) For achieving a just settlement of the refugee problem;

(c) For guaranteeing the territorial inviolability and political independence of every State in the area, through measures including the establishment of demilitarized zones;

3. *Requests* the Secretary-General to designate a Special Representative to proceed to the Middle East to establish and maintain contacts with the States concerned in order to promote agreement and assist efforts to achieve a peaceful and accepted settlement in accordance with the provisions and principles in this resolution;

4. *Requests* the Secretary-General to report to the Security Council on the progress of the efforts of the Special Representative as soon as possible.

Meaning of the Security Council Resolution

Security Council Resolution 242 of November 22, 1967, would appear to contain all the elements of a satisfactory solution of the Arab-Israeli problem. It was accepted by all members of the Security Council, by all the Arab neighbors of Israel with the possible exception of Syria, and—with serious qualifications—by Israel, but it has not been implemented.[15] The resolution assumes the continued

[15] The position of the Palestine Arab delegation before the Special Political Committee of the General Assembly, presented in 1969, is extreme. It calls for repatriation of the Arab refugees and Jewish immigrants to their respective places of origin, nullification of the United Nations partition resolution, elimination of the present state of Israel, and self-determination of Palestine as an Arab state. See *United Nations Monthly Chronicle,* June 1969, pp. 83-84.

existence of Israel and the Arab states and applies principles and procedures recognized by customary and conventional international law, especially by the United Nations Charter, to establish and maintain peaceful relations among contending states. It affirms:

(1) The legal prohibition of war, force and threat in international relations,

(2) The right of *states* to territorial integrity, political independence and the exercise of domestic jursidiction, and consideration of the claims of *peoples* to self-determination,

(3) The distinction between occupation of, and title to, territory, and the prohibition of force for acquiring the latter and establishing boundaries,

(4) Rights of navigation in international straits and canals,

(5) The obligation of states in respect to refugees from their territories.

The first three of these issues will be considered in detail in the following sections. The other two, navigation rights and the refugee problem, are touched on briefly here and treated in depth in following chapters.

War or Peace? The Use of Force in International Relations. The first thing to note about Security Council Resolution 242 of November 22, 1967, is the third paragraph of its preamble, in which the Security Council emphasizes "that all member states in their acceptance of the Charter of the United Nations have undertaken a commitment to act in accordance with Article 2 of the Charter." Article 2 of the United Nations Charter provides that the members shall act in accordance with a number of "Principles," including the following:

"All Members shall settle their international disputes by peaceful means in such a manner that international peace and security, and justice, are not endangered" (Section 3); and

"All Members shall refrain in their international relations from the threat or use of force against the territorial integrity or political independence of any state. . . ." (Section 4).

It is argued by Professor Quincy Wright that the Charter thus amplifies the obligations of the parties to the Kellogg-Briand Pact of 1928, enforced by the Nuremberg and other war crimes tribunals after World War II "to renounce [war] as an instrument of national policy in their relations with one another" and "never to seek settlement of disputes or conflicts which arise among them except by pacific means." Wright maintains that these provisions of the Charter and the Kellogg-Briand Pact are designed to "outlaw war" in the legal sense of a situation in which the belligerents have an equal right to engage in hostilities and other coercive actions permissible under the law of war, and in which other states are obliged to observe the law of neutrality requiring impartiality. Under a strict interpretation of the Charter, therefore, it can be argued that a "state of war" cannot exist between members of the United Nations or—according to Article 2, Section 6, which says that the U.N. shall ensure that nonmember states act in interpretation of the Charter, therefore, it can be argued that a "state of war" implies a continuing use or threat of force by each belligerent upon the other and equality between the belligerents. In the two circumstances in which the Charter permits use of force in international relations—self-defense and collective security action—the belligerents are not equal. The defenders and the states cooperating with the United Nations enjoy rights denied the aggressor. Other states need not be neutral but may assist the defender in "collective self-defense" (Article 51), and "shall give the United Nations every assistance" in action against an aggressor (Article 2, Section 5).[16]

Professor Wright therefore holds that the reference in the preamble of Resolution 242 to Article 2 of the Charter imports a positive obligation of international law which the parties must "fulfill in good faith" (Article 2, Section 2). Moreover, he points to the first operative paragraph of the resolution, in which the Security Council "affirms that the fulfillment of Charter principles requires the establishment of a just and lasting peace in the Middle East which should include the application of both the following principles: . . . (ii) Termination of all claims or states of belligerency. . . ." The argument, in short, is that these documents require the states involved to be in a "state of peace" rather than a "state of war," and that any contrary view conflicts with the requirements of international law.[17]

Other international lawyers contend that this analysis, however well intended in the interest of promoting international peace, is insufficient. In developing their position they rely heavily on the course of Arab-Israeli relations since 1947-48. From a legal standpoint the issue is significant, for the existence or nonexistence of a state of belligerency is a basic point of departure for the evaluation of many other related legal problems. Put briefly, if a state of war continues to exist, it provides a reasonable legal defense against a party seeking to invoke the law of peace in the settlement of such issues.

The 1949 Armistice Agreements. Following the 1948-49 hostilities, Israel took the position that peace had been established by virtue of the armistice agreements reached in the spring of 1949; the Arabs maintained that these agreements terminated hostile actions but not the state of war. The Arabs refused to grant Israel recognition, on the ground that the new nation had been established in a territory against the wishes of the people who inhabited that territory. It was also charged that Israel had taken private property by force without consent or compensation. Assuming normal peaceful relations, a state is entitled to establish diplomatic. and trade relations, and its citizens are entitled to move freely across frontiers. The Arabs, by insisting that a state of war persisted, sought legal justification for denying such rights and privileges to Israel.

In evaluating the Arab position it should be recalled that over the years since 1948 Israel has frequently resorted to military measures of various kinds, and twice (in 1956 and 1967) has involved itself in full-scale armed conflict with its Arab neighbors. Moreover, in each of the Arab-Israeli conflicts *both sides* have

---

[16] Quincy Wright, "The Meaning of the Pact of Paris," *American Journal of International Law,* vol. 27 (1933), pp. 209ff.; Wright, "The Law of the Nuremberg Trial," ibid., vol. 41 (1947), pp. 62ff.; Wright, "The Outlawry of War and the Law of War," ibid., vol. 47 (1953), p. 365.

[17] Wright, "Legal Aspects of the Middle East Situation," *Law and Contemporary Problems,* vol. 33 (1968).

invoked their "inherent right" of self-defense under Article 51 of the United Nations Charter, an action which by its very nature tends to negate the concept of a state of peace. It is true that under accepted canons of international law the bare commission of acts of international violence does not always suffice to bring about a state of war; it is equally true that a state of war may exist prior to the use of force and may continue to exist after fighting has ceased. A state of war may occur when one state manifests an intention not to allow its relationship with another to be governed by the laws of peace; it is brought into being by an act terminating the condition of peace.

As stated by Julius Stone, such a manifestation may take the form of "commission of some act of force by one party intended to terminate legal relations of peace between the parties [or such an act] even if that first party had no such intent, if the other elects to treat the act of force as being done with that intent."[18]

As stated by Kelsen: "War may be considered to begin upon the communication of a declaration of war, or through the proclamation of a state that it considers itself to be at war with another state." [19]

In other words, war begins by an act regarded by either party in a bilateral relationship as constituting war. A state of war can exist even if the assertion of belligerency is only unilateral; it ends only when both parties consider themselves at peace. The actions and intentions of states, taken together, determine whether war exists. Professor Kelsen, in discussing peace treaties, has written:"If the government of one belligerent, in violation of the peace treaty, should continue to perform acts of war, the war would not be terminated. Hence it is not . . . by the peace treaty, it is rather by carrying out the obligation stipulated in the peace treaty that the belligerents terminate the war." [20]

The Armistice Agreements of 1949, even though accompanied by termination of hostilities, are not peace treaties. In fact, Egypt deliberately pursued a policy designed to avoid legitimizing the territorial status quo of 1949. The refusal of the Arabs to enter into peace talks in 1949 is the clearest evidence that they were not prepared at that time to declare themselves at peace with Israel. They have consistently maintained this position. Israel, on the other hand, regarded the Egypt-Israeli armistice agreement, the most important of the four agreements, as more than a mere suspension of hostilities. Its spokesmen described the armistice as a permanent, irrevocable renunciation of all hostile acts, and pointed to the agreement's provision (Article XII, section 2) that it was to remain in force until a peaceful settlement was achieved. In view of these conflicting positions, further examination of the armistice agreement is in order. [21]

The language of the preamble indicates the context in which the agreement was negotiated: "a further provisional measure . . . in order to facilitate the transition from the present truce to permanent peace." The armistice was negotiated in an effort to set up arrangements which would preclude military operations and

---

[18] Julius Stone, *Legal Controls of International Conflict* (New York, 1954), p. 310.
[19] Hans Kelsen, *Principles of International Law,* 2nd ed. (New York, 1966), p. 91.
[20] Ibid., p. 96.
[21] Text in Hurewitz, *Diplomacy,* vol. II, pp. 299-304.

provide an environment within which there could be movement toward a political settlement. It is certainly arguable, as the Arabs have argued, that the four 1949 armistice agreements were of a provisional, incomplete and military nature, and were not intended by the parties to end the state of war or to proscribe the exercise of all belligerent rights. In the Egypt-Israeli agreement, for instance, one can point to the prohibition of the passage of military or para-military forces through waters within three miles of the other party's coast (Article II), a significant qualification upon the right of free and innocent passage which ordinarily applies to coastal waters under conditions of peace.

Arabs have maintained that while Article XII, section 2 of the agreement stipulated that it should remain in force until achievement of a peaceful settlement, the intention of this provision, when read together with other clauses of the agreement, was to freeze the military situation and guard against a renewal of fighting. Political factors that had given rise to the state of belligerency were to be dealt with in the final peace settlement. Since the four armistice agreements were conceived as a platform to sustain the erection of a larger political structure of peace, they were not designed to stand alone after efforts to complete a peace regime had been abandoned.

A key element of the Arab position has been that the 1949 armistice agreements did not extinguish all belligerent rights. The relations of Israel and its Arab neighbors were originally those of war; since 1949 it is apparent that the normal international condition of peace has not been in effect. Nonmilitary manifestations of belligerency such as the blockade of Israeli shipping, not being proscribed by the armistice agreements, are defended by the Arabs as legitimate. Of course the very assertion of such belligerent rights has lent substance to the condition of belligerency—and has stimulated retaliation.[22]

Professor Wright takes a different view on this question.[23] The outlawing of war by the United Nations Charter, he maintains, means not only that armed force may not be used as an instrument of foreign policy but also that other powers of belligerents, permissible during a "state of war," such as blockades, property confiscations, visit and search at sea, and so on, are not permissible. He seriously questions the Arab argument that the armistice agreements of 1949, while forbidding use of armed force contrary to their terms, allowed the exercise of other belligerent powers, such as blockade of the Suez Canal against Israeli shipping. The armistices, he contends, were to end de facto, but illegal, hostilities and to establish temporary lines of occupation; they did not recognize a "state of war"; neither side enjoyed belligerent powers. Furthermore, he challenges, as being inconsistent with the obligations of the Arab states under the Charter, an argument sometimes advanced by Arabs that the "state of war" with Israel came into existence with partition before Israel was a state or a member of the United

---

[22] For elaboration of the Arab position, see statement by George Tomeh, Permanent Representative of Syria at the United Nations, in *Law and Contemporary Problems,* vol. 33 (1968), pp. 120ff.; Cherif Bassiouni, "Some Legal Aspects of the Arab-Israeli Conflict," *The Arab World* (Special Issue, New York, 1968), pp. 41ff.; statement by Egyptian Ambassador El Kony at the Security Council, May 29, 1967, reproduced in *International Organization,* vol. 21 (Autumn 1967), pp. 940ff.

[23] Wright, "Legal Aspects," *supra,* note 17.

Nations, and will continue until conclusion of peace treaties. Wright points out that none of the international hostilities which have occurred since World War II, including those in the Middle East, have been generally recognized as a state of war in the legal sense, although those of considerable magnitude such as Korea (1950-53), Vietnam (1965-   ) and Middle East (1967) have been referred to as "war" in the vernacular.

In its resolution of September 1, 1951, relating to transit through the Suez Canal,[24] the Security Council declared that since the armistice regime was of a permanent character, the parties to it could not reasonably assert that they were active belligerents or that the exercise of belligerent rights was permissible or required; accordingly, Egypt's restrictive policy regarding the passage of shipping through the Suez Canal represented "unjustified interference with the rights of nations to navigate the seas and trade freely." (The Suez Canal question is treated more fully in Chapter IV.) The legal basis for this resolution has been questioned. As one commentator has written: "It is more likely that the Security Council's action was based upon a desire to end a dangerous situation rather than an attempt to change a long-established rule of international law." [25]

On November 3, 1956, following its invasion of Sinai, the government of Israel, in an aide memoire addressed to the secretary-general of the United Nations, denounced the Egypt-Israeli armistice agreement as a "fiction"; Egypt's policy of "murderous attacks" and "relentless siege" had "destroyed the armistice agreement." Since the agreement had been construed to allow continuance of a state of war, Israel stated that it now sought "establishment of peace by direct negotiations." By this time, it can be argued, Israel recognized the existence of a de facto state of war, at least between Israel and Egypt. Since then Israel has continued to call for the establishment of peace by direct negotiations.

To many Arab diplomats and jurists the proposition that the United Nations charter unconditionally prohibits a state of war seems strained and unrealistic. They do not agree that the 1949 armistice agreements terminated the state of belligerency. And indeed some authorities hold that insistence on these propositions in the abstract tends to obscure the real issues that must be faced on the road to peace, and that failure to concede the existence of a state of war of intermittent intensity since 1948 discounts unnecessarily the work of the United Nations and the efforts of the Great Powers to deal with the situation through its mechanism. In their view, arguments of this nature may harden further the already rigid policies of the opposing parties, and inhibit rather than enhance understanding of the very real and very deep conflicts of interest and ideology which agitate the antagonists in the present Middle East crisis.

The Fedayeen. While the United Nations charter calls upon all states to refrain from the use of force in international relations except in defense against armed attack, the charter prohibition does not apply to civil strife. The situation of the irregular forces known as fedayeen must therefore be considered. To the

---

[24] Text in Laqueur, *The Israeli-Arab Reader,* pp. 136-37; see also Magnus, *Documents on the Middle East,"* pp. 164-65.

[25] Howard S. Levie, "The Nature and Scope of the Armistice Agreement," *American Journal of International Law,* vol. 50 (1956), p. 886.

extent that any Arab state encourages these forces or permits them to operate from its territory against Israel, it runs afoul of its Charter obligations; Israel is justified in taking defensive action, although excessive retaliation upon Arab villages cannot be justified, and has been condemned by the Security Council on a number of occasions.

Since the hostilities of 1967, however, the activities of the Arab guerrillas or partisans have to an increasing extent been organized under the direction of the "Palestine Liberation Organization" composed of Palestinian Arabs who appear to have refused to recognize the partition of Palestine. They claim the status of "insurgents," functioning within the area occupied by Israel to establish the unity of Palestine as an Arab state within the boundaries defined in the mandate.

"Insurgency" has long been recognized in international law as the status of rebels or revolutionaries acting, within a state's territory or upon its ships at sea, to change its government or to secede, with such effectiveness that the result of the civil strife is uncertain. As long as neither faction interferes with the rights of outside states on the high seas or elsewhere and receives no military assistance from outside, the hostilities are within the domestic jurisdiction of the state where they occur and other states are obliged not to intervene.[26]

The insurgency of the Confederate States of America was recognized as "belligerency," as were several previous instances of "insurgency," and it was often said that if civil hostilities were of large magnitude, and extended to naval operations affecting outside states, such recognition, according full belligerent powers to both the insurgents and the government, and requiring outside states to observe the obligations of neutrality, was permissible or even obligatory. Since the American Civil War, however, belligerency has seldom if ever been recognized in situations of civil strife and would appear to be inconsistent with the anti-war obligations of parties to the U.N. Charter and other instruments, as well as generally contrary to the interests of states to prevent a broadening of the area of hostilities and interference with their commerce on the high seas. Large scale civil or colonial hostilities such as those in the Philippines (1899-1901), Spain (1936-39), Algeria (1957-62), Vietnam (1947-54), Congo (1960-62), and Nigeria (1966-70) have not been recognized as belligerency.

The law of war as codified in the Hague Convention of 1899 and 1907 (Article 1) and the Geneva Convention on Prisoners of War of 1949 (Article 4) recognizes that militia and volunteer corps are entitled to treatment as belligerents if they are commanded by responsible persons, if they wear a distinctive symbol recognizable at a distance, if they bear arms openly, and if they observe the laws of war. These conventions go further in recognizing that the "inhabitants of a territory which has not been occupied, who on the approach of the enemy

---

[26] W. E. Hall, *A Treatise on International Law*, 8th ed. (Oxford, 1924), p. 347; George Grafton Wilson, *Handbook of International Law* (St. Paul, Minn., 1910), p. 62; Quincy Wright, "United States Intervention in the Lebanon," *American Journal of International Law*, vol. 53 (1959), p. 121; Wright, "International Law and Civil Strife," *Proceedings of the American Society of International Law* (1959), p. 148. John Norton Moore has suggested four criteria for the existence of insurgency and certain circumstances permitting intervention during civil strife: "The Control of Foreign Intervention in Internal Conflict," *The Virginia Journal of International Law*, vol. 9 (1969), p. 337.

spontaneously take up arms to resist the invading troops without having had time to organize" have the same status if they observe the last two of these criteria. It would appear, however, that Israel occupied the areas within the cease-fire lines of 1967 sufficiently so that the military activity of the inhabitants would not be a *levee en masse* in this sense. The Palestine Liberation Organization has subsequently increased its effectiveness and may by now be entitled to the status of insurgency. It is clearly acting for a political purpose and, if its forces are operating within the occupied territory with such effectiveness that the results are uncertain and if they conform to the requirements of militia or volunteer corps, they are insurgents entitled to treatment according to the law of war including the rights of prisoners of war if captured.[27]

The Hague and Geneva conventions apply the humanitarian rules of war to forces of states, parties to the conventions, whether or not engaged in formal war. Customary international law, however, applies these rules during insurgency, and the Geneva Conventions of 1949 go further in explicitly applying many of them to all forces engaged in civil strife even if they lack the status of insurgents. Assassinations, attacks on civilians, and other acts in violation of the law of war, committed by forces either of the Palestine Liberation Organization or Israel, are war crimes, subject to punishment under the principles of the Nuremberg Charter. It would appear that the forces of the Palestine Liberation Organization, insofar as they conform to the criteria of the Hague and Geneva conventions, should be treated according to the humanitarian rules of war; and outside states, including the Arab states, should neither assist them nor intervene against them as long as they operate within territory bounded by the cease-fire lines of 1967.

Territorial Integrity, Political Independence, and Self-Determination. The Security Council resolution demands "respect for and acknowledgement of the sovereignty, territorial integrity and political independence of every state in the area." It thus affirms the basic commitments of the United Nations Charter, "the sovereign equality of all members," respect for their territorial integrity and political independence and freedom from intervention, even by the United Nations, in "matters which are essentially within their domestic jurisdiction."

These legal principles must be distinguished from the political principles of the Charter calling for the "self-determination of peoples" and affirmed in the anti-colonial declaration and in the human rights covenants approved by the General Assembly in 1960 and 1966 respectively. Self-determination means that a people similar in culture, aspiration or geographical position should be given the opportunity to decide whether they want to become an independent state. This principle has been utilized to effect the emancipation of colonies and to transfer territories in accord with the result of plebiscites. The normal subjects of international law, however, are not "peoples" but "states." The recognition of a distinctive people, whether within a colony or the home territory of a state, or scattered throughout the world, is inconsistent with the rights of the state within whose

---

[27] On this point, illustrative articles by informed journalists include Alfred Friendly in the *Washington Post,* Nov. 22, 1969; Rowland Evans and Robert Novak in the *Washington Post,* Nov. 20, 1969.

territory they live. Such recognition involves political and legal change but, in accord with the Charter, must not involve the use of force by outside states.

The Charter, however, although assuming that such changes normally require the acquiescence of the territorial state, considers pressures by internal groups demanding their self-determination, even by revolutionary means, as a domestic question with which outside states may not interfere. It is the state, not the government, that must acquiesce. The internal process by which such acquiescence is obtained, whether constitutional or revolutionary, whether by the permission or the replacement of the government, is a matter within the state's domestic jurisdiction. The Charter goes further in facilitating peaceful change by authorizing the General Assembly to "recommend measures for the peaceful adjustment of any situation" in order to realize the purposes of the Charter such as the self-determination of peoples (Article 14) and even authorizes the Security Council to make binding decisions to this end, in case demands for self-determination threaten international peace and the council considers such decision necessary "to maintain or to restore international peace and security" (Article 39).

The Balfour Declaration and the Palestine Mandate, in recognizing the Jewish people as entitled to a national home in Palestine because of historical connection, were political decisions difficult to reconcile with the claim of the Arab population to self-determination. Nevertheless, they would have become legally valid if generally recognized and acquiesced in for many years, prior to partition, by the Arab population and the mandatory government of Palestine, and by Arab states.

Similarly, the United Nations partition resolution of November 29, 1947, was difficult to reconcile with the provisional recognition of Palestine as a state in the League of Nations Covenant (Article 22) and the provision in the United Nations Charter (Article 80) that nothing in the Charter concerning trusteeships "shall be construed in and of itself to alter in any manner the rights whatsoever of any state or any peoples or the terms of existing instruments to which members of the United Nations may respectively be parties." Partition of Palestine violated rights of the Arab peoples of Palestine, explicitly protected by the mandate, and of the Arab states, parties to the United Nations Charter and also of the League of Nations Covenant establishing the status of the Palestine Mandate.

Partition could only be justified as a political decision to maintain international peace and security after Great Britain, the mandatory, had transferred its powers and responsibilities to the United Nations General Assembly and Palestine was facing de facto hostilities. Like the Balfour Declaration, partition, at least within the boundaries defined by the United Nations resolution of November 1947, corresponded in some degree to self-determination in accord with the distribution of the Jewish and Arab populations at that time. It achieved legal validity by the general recognition of Israel and its admittance to the United Nations. Territorial boundaries, however, beyond those in the resolution were not established. Israel remained merely a de facto occupant of the territories within the cease-fire lines of 1949 and 1967. The continuous objection of the Palestinian Arabs and the surrounding Arab states prevented Israel from acquiring title to the occupied territories either by the principle of prescription or the principle of general recognition.[28]

The inherent conflict between political changes to effect the self-determination of peoples and legal titles to territory has not been resolved. It constitutes a basic cause of actual or cold war in the Middle East since partition.

Establishment of Boundaries. The preamble of the Security Council's resolution emphasizes "the inadmissibility of the acquisition of territory by war and the need to work for a just and lasting peace in which every state in the area can live in security." To this end, states the resolution, and in accord with their commitments under Article 2 of the United Nations Charter, the states in the area must apply the principles of "withdrawal of Israeli armed forces from territories occupied in the recent [1967] conflict" and "termination of all claims or states of belligerency and respect for and acknowledgement of the sovereignty, territorial integrity, and political independence of every state in the area and their right to live in peace within secure and recognized boundaries free from threats or acts of force." The resolution also calls upon the secretary-general to send a special representative to the area "to promote agreement and assist efforts to achieve a peaceful and accepted settlement in accordance with the provisions and principles in this resolution." The resolution does not indicate how boundaries are to be established, though it makes clear that they must not be established by force.

The principle of the "inadmissibility of the acquisition of territory by war" goes beyond the principle "no fruits of aggression." It says there shall be no territorial fruits from war, the latter term being interpreted in the material sense of a considerable use of armed force, even by a state acting in self-defense. Its application, therefore, does not depend on determining who was the "aggressor" in the 1967 hostilities. Whether or not Israel was the aggressor, its occupation of territory was achieved by the use of armed force and is therefore "inadmissible." This principle is well established. It is inherent in the rules of customary international law defining "military occupation" and permitting acquisition of occupied territory only by annexation following generally recognized "completed conquest," i.e., cession by the former sovereign or prescription or adjudication. It was accepted, in the form "no title by conquest," as a principle of American international law by most of the members of the Pan-American Conference of 1890. It was assumed in President Wilson's Fourteen Points and was generally applied in the peace settlements of World War I, which usually required plebiscites to justify territorial transfers. It was assumed by the League of Nations and asserted in the Geneva Protocol of 1925. It was particularly insisted upon in the Stimson Doctrine, whereby the United States refused to recognize any Japanese acquisitions by its invasion and occupation of Manchuria in 1931. Secretary of State Stimson considered it an implication of the Kellogg-Briand Pact of 1928 to which the United States, though not a member of the league, was a party. By this pact nearly all states renounced war as an instrument of national policy. The pact provided the legal bases for the crime against peace in the Nuremberg trials and other war crimes trials after World War II. The League of Nations accepted the Stimson

---

[28] Wright, "The Middle East Crisis," pp. 22-23.

Doctrine as a necessary implication of Article 10 of the covenant guaranteeing the territorial integrity of all members of the league. The United States insisted on this principle in the Atlantic Charter of 1941, before its entry into World War II, and in the settlements after the war. The Allies, it is true, made some territorial acquisitions as a result of their victory but sought to justify them, not very successfully in all cases, on the principle of self-determination of peoples. The principle of "no title by conquest" has been considered an implication of the United Nations Charter obligation (Article 2, paragraph 4) to refrain from the use or threat of force against the territorial integrity of any state.[29]

It is worth reviewing how this principle has been applied in the Arab-Israeli situation:

(a) As noted in the preceding section, the United Nations General Assembly resolution of November 29, 1947, partitioning Palestine and establishing the state of Israel (as demanded by Zionists supported by hostilities of local terrorists) is difficult to reconcile with the principle. It was probably, however, eventually validated by the principle of general recognition inasmuch as Israel was admitted to the United Nations on May 11, 1949, and on the next day the Arab states signed the Lausanne protocol provisionally accepting the partition resolution as the basis for negotiating permanent boundaries.[30]

(b) The extension of Israel's occupation beyond the original United Nations grant was a result of the Arab-Israeli hostilities of 1948-49 and of the armistices based on existing lines of occupation, negotiated in 1949 between Israel and its Arab neighbors through the mediation of Ralph Bunche as United Nations agent. These new boundaries are difficult to justify. The principle of no acquisition of territory by war should, strictly applied, require that cease-fire lines be at the frontiers before hostilities began, thus preventing military occupations as well as territorial acquisitions by force. The overriding responsibility of the United Nations to stop hostilities necessitated the armistices, but only as temporary cease-fire lines to be soon superseded by permanent boundaries established by peaceful means.

(c) In the hostilities of 1956, the principle was strictly adhered to. France, Britain, and Israel, under pressure of the General Assembly, supported by the U.S. and the U.S.S.R., were induced to withdraw to their positions before the hostilities.

---

[29] Shabtai Rosenne, an Israeli diplomat, gives other instances in which the principle was applied, but seeks to qualify the Security Council's demand for the "withdrawal of Israeli armed forces from territory occupied in the recent conflict," on the ground that preliminary drafts of the resolution, "the intent of which was to require withdrawal, immediately or otherwise, of all Israeli forces back to the lines they occupied on June 5, 1967," were rejected by the Security Council. See his statement in *Law and Contemporary Problems*, vol. 33 (1968), at p. 59. See also views of John W. Halderman, ibid., p. 89. Cf. Bassiouni, "Arab-Israeli Conflict," *supra*, note 22, at p. 44. There is a table indicating the results in 78 political disputes before the United Nations in Quincy Wright, "Peace-Keeping Operations of the United Nations," *International Studies* (Indian School of International Studies), vol. 7 (1965), p. 176.

[30] Reports of the Conciliation Commission, June 13, 1949, Sept. 22, 1949, and Sept. 2, 1950, *General Assembly Official Records* IV. Ad Hoc Political Committee, Annex, vol. II, pp. 5-13; V. Supp. 18, A/1367/Rev. 1, pp. 2-21, referred to in Louis Sohn, *Cases on United Nations Law* (1961), at p. 472. The ambiguities of this document are noted in Pablo de Azcarate, *Mission in Palestine, 1948-1952* (Washington: Middle East Institute, 1966).

(d) The circumstances inducing the Security Council to accept cease-fires in June and July 1967 on the lines of Israel occupation were similar to those of 1949. The Security Council resolutions were justified as necessary to end hostilities, but could not be regarded as conferring upon Israel any rights to the territory it occupied. It is unfortunate from the legal standpoint that the position taken in 1956, requiring Israel immediately to withdraw to its de facto frontiers before the hostilities, was not adhered to in 1967.[31] If the U.S. and the U.S.S.R., supported by France and Great Britain (as they had not been in 1956), had insisted in the Security Council, with support of the General Assembly, upon immediate withdrawal, it might have been effected. The American preoccupation with Vietnam and its opposition to the Soviet Union on this problem, as well as American concern for domestic political considerations, were probably factors preventing the adoption of a common position as was taken by the superpowers and the United Nations in 1956.

In any case, the principle in question clearly requires that Israel gain no political advantage, in respect to the establishment of permanent boundaries with its Arab neighbors, by its occupation of Egyptian, Jordanian, and Syrian territories. No one can doubt that Israel would have a political advantage if it negotiated bilaterally on boundaries with each of these neighbors while it occupied territories in dispute.

To recapitulate: the principle of no territorial acquisitions by force is not only sanctioned by general treaties, such as the League Covenant, the Kellogg-Briand Pact and the United Nations Charter, but also by customary international law developed by state practices during the nineteenth century. Together with the prohibition in international relations of the use of force by states except in self-defense, it is not only an effective instrument to realize the purpose to which governments have committed themselves, but it may well be the very price of their survival—"to save succeeding generations from the scourge of war." This purpose is not likely to be realized as long as war in the material sense or the use of armed forces can, in some circumstances, be used as an instrument of foreign policy and especially of territorial expansions. It has always been recognized that the use of force or duress to induce a settlement renders the settlement unstable if not invalid.[32] "Peace treaties" providing for territorial cessions enforced by the victor have frequently been short-lived. They have often stimulated later war to recover the ceded territory. Since World War II it has been widely recognized that the danger that international hostilities will escalate to nuclear war, and that hostilities against guerrillas are likely to continue with increasing barbarism, have further reduced the usefulness of war or military intervention in

---

[31] See Quincy Wright, "Intervention, 1956," *American Journal of International Law,* vol. 51 (1957), p. 257.

[32] The Vienna Convention on the Law of Treaties, 1969, provides not only that a state's consent to a treaty is ineffective if procured by coercion (Article 51), but also that a "treaty is void if procured by the threat or use of force in violation of principles of international law embodied in the Charter of the United Nations" (Article 52). Text in *American Journal of International Law,* vol. 63 (1969), p. 891. For critical comments on similar provisions in the International Law Commission drafts on the subject, see Julius Stone, "De Victoribus Victis: The International Law Commission and Enforced Treaties of Peace," *Virginia Journal of International Law,* vol. 8 (1968), p. 85.

the conduct of foreign policy and imperial expansion. Hostilities of considerable magnitude have occurred, it is true, over 40 times since World War II. Most of them were instances of civil strife or colonial revolt within the domestic jurisdiction of a state, generally resulting in the success of the rebels. Most of the remainder were ended by a cease-fire arranged by the United Nations or some other international agency without gain to either belligerent (only, it is true, after large-scale hostilities in the case of Korea in 1950). The Soviet interventions in Hungary (1956) and Czechoslovakia (1968), the U.S. intervention in Vietnam (1965), the Chinese invasion of India (1962), and the Indian occupation of Goa (1961), were not stopped by a United Nations cease-fire. But only in the last case, which involved minor hostilities, did the intervening state appear to have gained territory or much political advantage.[33] Apart from its use by genuine defenders against armed attack and by colonial peoples seeking self-determination, armed force has not proved of much value in the nuclear age. Because of this experience and because of the increased availability of collective diplomacy, propaganda, economic assistance, trade controls, and other nonmilitary instruments in the conduct of foreign policy, the latter methods have usually seemed preferable alternatives to the use of armed force.[34]

Aside from technical conditions limiting the utility of armed force in international relations, if the community of nations led by the United Nations should regularly employ positive measures to thwart territorial or other political advantages which a state may hope to gain by the use of armed force, the utility of military aggression might be reduced to near zero. There is, therefore, a practical reason as well as a legal reason for preventing acquisition of title by the use of armed force.

If this principle is maintained, how may Arab-Israeli boundaries be established? Theoretically, there are several possibilities that would be consistent with customary international law, the United Nations Charter (Article 33),[35] and Security Council Resolution 242: (1) agreement of the parties not involving duress; (2) prescription by long acquiescence of the adverse claimant in a de facto boundary; (3) general recognition of such a boundary by most states of the world; and (4) decision of the United Nations Security Council, the International Court of Justice, an arbitral tribunal, or other body given authority by the parties to make a decision. Prescription is hardly realistic in the Middle East situation because of the continued refusal of the Arab states to acquiesce in the cease-fire lines of either 1949 or 1967 as boundaries, and there is not likely to be general recognition of these lines. The problem, therefore, becomes one of applying some combination of (1) and (4)—that is, achieving agreement between Israel and its neighbors by negotiation, directly under conditions preventing duress, through

---

[33] Wright, "Peace-Keeping Operations," *supra,* note 29.

[34] Wright, *A Study of War,* 2d ed. (Chicago, 1965), pp. 1518ff.

[35] Article 33 of the United Nations Charter states:

"1. The parties to any dispute, the continuance of which is likely to endanger the maintenance of international peace and security, shall, first of all, seek a solution by negotiation, enquiry, mediation, conciliation, arbitration, judicial settlement, resort to regional agencies or arrangements, or other peaceful means of their own choice.

2. The Security Council shall, when it deems necessary, call upon the parties to settle their dispute by such means."

mediators or conciliators, or by award of some forum given power by the parties to decide on a boundary.

No agreement on boundaries has yet been reached. Israel apparently will not withdraw from occupied territories until convinced that the Arab states have renounced belligerency and recognized Israel as a sovereign state, and Israel apparently will not be convinced that they have done so until they have agreed on permanent boundaries. The Arab states, on the other hand, will not negotiate on boundaries until Israel has withdrawn, at least from the territories occupied in 1967.

To many, the action called for by Article 1 of the Security Council resolution (see above for text) seems tolerably clear. The Arab states, at least Egypt, Lebanon and Jordan, have declared that they accept it in full, thus implying that they are ready to renounce belligerency and recognize Israel as soon as the latter has withdrawn from the territory occupied in 1967. Israel, however, has attempted to interpret the phrase "from territories occupied in the recent conflict" as not including *all* such territories.[36] Israel, moreover, has professed to annex all of Jerusalem and has said that it will not withdraw from this and other occupied areas such as the Golan Heights in Syrian territory, portions of Sinai in Egyptian territory, and the Gaza Strip. The Security Council could, if the five permanent members were in agreement, break the deadlock by reaffirming that the resolution means what it says, and that Israel must withdraw from all the territories occupied in the 1967 hostilities. This is the requirement of international law, the Charter, and the resolution; and it is probably essential if the further steps toward securing peace — those concerning determination of boundaries, navigation of waterways, just settlement of the refugee problem, and suitable guarantees — are to be taken. Even if accepted in principle, however, the first step presents difficulties in arranging stages of withdrawal, supervision, and timing in relation to Israel's security requirements and Arab renunciation of force and recognition of Israel.

In view of the Arab acceptance of the Resolution, Israel's refusal to do so without important qualifications, including refusal to agree on withdrawal from certain occupied territories, clearly puts her on the defensive diplomatically and legally. Part of the difficulty might be resolved by providing that the occupied territories, or at least those portions deemed most critical by Israel, should not be reoccupied by Arab states upon Israel's withdrawal, but rather by the United Nations. There is a precedent for such a formula in the procedure used in dealing with the West Irian problem. West Irian is the western part of the island of New Guinea, just north of Australia, formerly controlled by the Netherlands. After hostilities had broken out between Dutch and Indonesian forces, agreement was reached in 1962 (with the aid of United Nations mediator Ellsworth Bunker) for evacuation of West Irian by both and administration by the United Nations for six months, after which Indonesia would occupy the area and prepare for its self-determination under United Nations supervision in 1969. A vote of tribal chiefs resulted in annexation of the area by Indonesia, a result not unexpected in view of

---

[36] Rosenne, *supra,* note 29.

Indonesian occupation at that time.[37] If a similar procedure were applied in the Middle East, it should be made clear that United Nations occupation should continue until the United Nations considers it no longer necessary; it should not be terminable at the discretion of the government claiming the territory (as was the United Nations occupation of the Egyptian boundary area from 1956 to 1967).

Solution of the problem of permanent boundaries and peace in the Middle East is a United Nations responsibility, inasmuch as Israel came into being under United Nations auspices. How may the United Nations discharge its responsibility to establish Israel's boundaries? It has been suggested that after the mutual renunciation of hostilities and withdrawal from occupied areas have been effected, as called for by the Security Council resolution of November 22, 1967, the United Nations might invite the parties to negotiate boundaries directly or with the aid of a mediator; but on the understanding that if agreement is not reached within a specified time (say one year), the boundary question should be referred to the Security Council or some other forum agreed on by the parties. This procedure would be similar to that by which the Mosul dispute between Turkey and Iraq (then under British Mandate) was settled in 1926. The Lausanne Treaty of 1924 provided that, if not settled by negotiation within a year, the league council would give a definitive decision on the boundaries between these two countries. When negotiations failed, the council awarded Mosul to Iraq under specific conditions.[38]

It should be understood that in the legal sense Israel has no generally recognized boundaries beyond those provided for in the original resolution of 1947. The armistice lines of 1949 and 1967 merely established cease-fire lines. The armistices of 1949, however, served as de facto boundaries for 20 years. Although not accepted by the Arabs, they were accorded certain recognition by the settlement after the Israeli invasion of 1956, and at all events they deserve greater consideration than the cease-fire lines of 1967. *Ex factis jus oritur.*

Among the forums which might be given the responsibility for settling the boundaries, if negotiation fails, are the Security Council acting under Article 38 (if the parties so request, the council may "make recommendations . . . with a view to a pacific settlement . . .") or the General Assembly acting under Article 14 (see above). In either case the agency must be granted the power (presumably with the acquiescence of the parties) not merely to recommend, but to *decide* the boundary. Another possible forum might be the International Court of Justice, if given authority by the parties to decide on the boundary *ex aequo et bono* as provided in Article 38, paragraph 2 of the court statute. It is clear that the deciding authority should not be limited by existing international law, but should be free to consider all the factors — political, economic, social, and cultural — which the parties might advance.

In territorial decisions the opinion of the inhabitants of the disputed territory has often been given much weight. Plebiscites have been arranged to determine their wishes in accord with the principle of self-determination of peoples. In view,

---

[37] See *Everyman's United Nations,* 8th ed. (1969), p. 124.

[38] Wright, "The Mosul Dispute," *American Journal of International Law,* vol. 20 (1926), p. 263.

however, of the movements — forced and voluntary — of the population of Palestine, the opinion of neither the present population nor that at any particular moment of history would seem appropriate. If the inhabitants of Palestine at the time of partition had been allowed to determine, Israel would have received no more, perhaps even less, territory than the original partition proposal, as suggested by Count Bernadotte's report made shortly before his assassination. If the present population were to determine, Israel would probably get most of the territory within the armistice lines of 1949 and perhaps some of the territory occupied in 1967. The fate of the plebiscite proposed for the Tacna-Arica area between Chile and Peru in 1925, when each was shipping in people to assure its victory in the plebiscite, illustrates the problem. (This boundary was finally settled by agreement of the parties.) [39] Claims, other than the wishes of the present or past population, would have to be considered in determining Israeli boundaries, as they were in the original partition resolution.

Another possible forum would be an *ad hoc* arbitral tribunal composed of neutral arbitrators. This was suggested as the final procedure by the General Act for the Pacfic Settlement of International Disputes, originally signed by 23 states under the auspices of the League of Nations in 1928, and brought up to date by the United Nations two decades later but signed then by only a few states.

Clearly the problem of establishing a forum acceptable to the parties would be difficult, whether before or after a period of negotiation, and would require considerable pressure by the Security Council and the Great Powers acting within it. United Nations occupation of the territory which Israel has occupied since 1967 would assist, especially if it implied responsibility of the United Nations to partition the occupied territory if the parties failed to agree either on a boundary or on a forum with power to decide. The extent to which the U.S. and U.S.S.R. could work in concert toward giving the United Nations such responsibilities is admittedly conjectural at this time.

In the context of boundaries the problem of Jerusalem presents special difficulties. The problem is an aspect of the general boundary question and could be dealt with in the way suggested above. As the General Assembly has already declared, Israel's annexation of Jerusalem is unacceptable.[40] Like the other territories occupied in 1967, eastern Jerusalem might be placed under United Nations control until a settlement is reached. The problem of Jerusalem is considered in detail in Chapter III.

Navigation of International Waterways. The rights to navigate in canals and straits have differed under international law. Navigation rights in canals depend on agreement with the state through whose territory the canal operates and navigation rights in straits depend on the international character of the strait.[41] If the 1967

---

[39] Wright, "The Tacna-Arica Dispute," *Minnesota Law Review,* vol. 10 (1925), p. 28.

[40] In *Jerusalem and the Holy Places* (London, 1968) at p. 50, Elihu Lauterpacht argues that Israel's action did not constitute "annexation."

[41] Majid Khadduri, "Closure of the Suez Canal to Israeli Shipping," *Law and Contemporary Problems,* vol. 33 (1968), pp. 152-53, citing Joseph A. Obeita, *The International Status of the Suez Canal* (The Hague, 1960). See also Wright, "Intervention, 1956," *supra,* note 31, at pp. 261ff.

Security Council resolution is implemented, Israel will have free access to the Suez Canal. It has been argued that the Constantinople Convention of 1888 made all states third party beneficiaries, assuring them the right of navigation in time of peace and war. This privilege has been enjoyed by the United States and many other nonparties to the convention. The Egyptian right of defense and responsibility to protect the canal are not unlimited. If Egypt wishes a stable peace it should be willing to accept, at least in principle, the United Nations resolution of 1951, supporting Israel's right to navigate the canal as provided for in the convention. In any case, Egypt presumably remains prepared to carry out its commitment of 1957 to submit all issues concerning the interpretation and application of the Constantinople convention to the International Court of Justice. (See Chapter IV.)

Israel's right of navigation in the Straits of Tiran and the Gulf of Aqaba, also called for by the resolution, has been disputed by the Arabs. Yet the Gulf appears to be a portion of the high seas because four states, including Israel, front on it. Under the Corfu Straits decision of the International Court of Justice and the Territorial Seas Convention of 1958, such waters are open to innocent passage of the vessels of all states. (For more detailed discussion, see Chapter IV.)

The Refugees. The rights of refugees depend upon the general principles in the Universal Declaration of Human Rights incorporated for the most part in the Covenants of Human Rights approved by the General Assembly in 1966 and to some extent in the conventions of 1933 and 1951 on the Status of Refugees. The Universal Declaration assures everyone of the right to life, liberty, and security of person; of freedom from arbitrary arrest, detention or exile; freedom of movement and residence within the borders of each state; freedom to leave any country including his own and to return to his country; and freedom to retain or change his nationality. These principles are converted into legal obligations by the customary international law forbidding states to deny justice to aliens within their territory and the rules of war protecting persons in occupied territory. According to the Hague Convention of 1907 which, in the main, codified the customary law of war, the occupant must respect the law pre-existing in the territory, refrain from compelling the inhabitants to give information about the enemy or his defenses or to take an oath of allegiance. The occupant must protect family honor, life, property and religious convictions, and give no general penalties for acts of individuals unless there is joint and several responsibility. The Geneva convention of 1949 provides more detailed rules to assure protection of civilians in occupied territory. These obligations to accord humane treatment to persons in national or occupied territory support the Security Council resolution of November 1967 "affirming the necessity for achieving a just settlement of the refugee problem." (For more detailed consideration, see Chapter III.)

Conclusion

Whatever the procedures utilized to implement the Security Council resolution, the results should be incorporated in a treaty signed by Israel and its Arab neighbors and placed under the guarantee of the United Nations and the permanent members of the Security Council. Separate agreements might be made in respect to the boundaries, the Suez Canal, the Gulf of Aqaba, the refugees and other issues, perhaps including the use of Jordan waters; but all should be guaranteed by the United Nations. It should be recognized that any complaint of violation of any of these agreements should immediately be placed before the Security Council, and if it failed to act because of a veto, the issue should go to the General Assembly as provided in the Uniting for Peace Resolution of 1950. This procedure proved effective in the hostilities of 1956.

Identifying the essential components of a "just and lasting peace" is a subjective process. As stated in the UNESCO Constitution, "It is in the minds of men that peace must be constructed." A Middle East settlement is not likely until the embittered and suspicious attitudes of Israel and its Arab neighbors have changed,[42] but such change will not be convincing to the other side until manifested by objective acts and utterances including full acceptance of the Security Council resolution of 1967. This requires formal recognition by Israel and its Arab neighbors that each enjoys the rights of a sovereign state, that each renounces belligerency and intends to evacuate territories occupied in 1967, that each accepts peaceful procedures to establish the boundaries of Israel, and that each intends to observe its obligations under Article 2 of the United Nations Charter.[43]

Both the Arab governments and the Palestine Liberation Organization may come to appreciate that force is more likely to induce general war than to restore Palestine as a whole to the Arabs. Both the Israeli government and the Zionists in all countries may come to appreciate first, that even if formal boundary agreements were signed as a result of territorial occupation or other coercion, they would not be likely to last; and second, that Israel, a small state in a large Arab

---

[42] Eliahu Elath, President of the Hebrew University in Jerusalem, former Israeli ambassador to the United States, in an address on "Jewish-Arab Relations in Israel" (March 29, 1967) suggests historic, economic and other factors that may improve these relations as well as relations between Israel and the Arab states. American Histadrut Cultural Exchange Institute, Pamphlet Series, no. 3, New York, 1967.

[43] The full text of Article 2 of the United Nations Charter reads:

"The Organization and its Members, in pursuit of the Purposes stated in Article 1, shall act in accordance with the following Principles:

1. The Organization is based on the principle of the sovereign equality of all its Members.

2. All Members, in order to insure to all of them the rights and benefits resulting from membership, shall fulfill in good faith the obligations assumed by them in accordance with the present Charter.

3. All Members shall settle their international disputes by peaceful means in such a manner that international peace and security, and justice, are not endangered.

4. All Members shall refrain in their international relations from the threat or use of force against the territorial integrity or political independence of any state, or in any other manner inconsistent with the Purposes of the United Nations.

5. All Members shall give the United Nations every assistance in any action it takes in accordance with the present Charter, and shall refrain from giving assistance to any state against which the United Nations is taking preventive or enforcement action.

6. The Organization shall ensure that states which are not Members of the United Nations act in accordance with these Principles so far as may be necessary for the maintenance of international peace and security.

7. Nothing contained in the present Charter shall authorize the United Nations to intervene in matters which are essentially within the domestic jurisdiction of any state or shall require the Members to submit such matters to settlement under the present Charter; but this principle shall not prejudice the application of enforcement measures under Chapter VII."

world, has a vital interest in peace with its neighbors. A "just and lasting peace" does not mean that all disputes have been settled, but it does mean that all parties are confident that only peaceful methods, such as stated in Article 33 [44] of the Charter, will be used to effect settlement. If the Security Council's resolution is implemented, the legacy of the Palestine conflict may be a lasting peace. If it is not, the legacy will probably be continued hostilities disastrous to the peoples of the area and perhaps to the world.

---

[44] See footnote 35 above for text of Article 33.

III. JERUSALEM,
THE OCCUPIED TERRITORIES,
AND THE REFUGEES

In considering the status of the areas occupied by Israel in the June War of 1967, it is important to distinguish between territories that were formerly part of Palestine and those that were not. In the former category are Jerusalem, the West Bank area of the Jordan River, and the Gaza Strip. In the latter are the Golan Heights of Syria and Egypt's Sinai Peninsula.

The emphasis in this chapter is on the former group, and most of all on Jerusalem, a focal point of concern for all interested parties to the Arab-Israeli dispute. Three main aspects of these problems are dealt with: the history of the movement to internationalize Jerusalem, the rules and standards of international law relating to belligerent occupation, and the legal claims of five principals—Israel, Jordan, the Arab states generally, the Palestinians, and the international community—with regard to any or all of the areas under consideration. The chapter concludes with a section on the Palestinian refugees.

Jerusalem: Background

The fact that for many centuries Jerusalem has been a focal point for three religions is, in and of itself, the underlying reason why there have been so many violent clashes in the Holy City and the Holy Land. For Jews, Zion (Jerusalem) is a symbol of their ancient heritage and a promise for the restoration of a Jewish state in Palestine. Indeed many Jews feel that a Jewish state without Jerusalem as its center would have little religious or political meaning. But Jerusalem is also central to Islam: Muhammad, according to the Koran, made a nocturnal trip to Jerusalem and the Holy Mosque (Masjid al-Aqsa) and then ascended into heaven.[1] Ever since the second caliph, Umar Ibn al-Khattab, accepted Byzantium's surrender of Jerusalem, shrines built there have made it the most important city for Muslims after Mecca and Medina. A magnificent mosque, the Dome of the Rock, was built on the spot where Muhammad was said to have led Muslims in prayer during his brief stay there. It happens that this very area, known as Haram al-Sharif, is where the ancient Jewish temple once stood. Many Muslims fear, rightly or wrongly, that under Israeli occupation this large enclosure, incorporating both the Masjid al-Aqsa and the Dome of the Rock, will be sacrificed to restore the temple. (The burning of the al-Aqsa mosque in August 1969 fanned this suspicion among Muslims in Palestine and elsewhere; since 1967 the area near the Wailing Wall, part of the western wall of Haram al-Sharif, has been cleared by Israeli authorities without disturbing the Muslim shrines themselves). To complicate matters further, Jerusalem of course has a key religious significance for Christians of all faiths in the immediate area and throughout the world.

---

[1] Koran, Chapter XVII.

Jerusalem's sovereignty has shifted many times. For four centuries, from 1517 to 1917, Palestine and Jerusalem were under the control of the Ottoman Empire. While the rights of the various religious groups were generally respected, many European Christians (and in due course American also) were dissatisfied with the rigidities of Ottoman rule. Beginning in the eighteenth century various European powers, including France, Russia, Britain and Austria, sought concessions from the sultan for the protection of Christians in the area and their shrines in and around Jerusalem. The Treaty of Paris, 1856, following the Crimean War, in effect provided international protection of the holy sites.[2]

As a result of the settlements following World War I, Britain was entrusted by the League of Nations with a mandate for Palestine, including Jerusalem. Hopes for the creation of one state, in which Arabs and Jews would cooperate through a representative form of government, gradually evaporated with the rise of competing Jewish and Arab nationalism. (See Chapter II.) The international community and Britain in particular endeavored to cope with the increasingly explosive situation. The Palestine mandate provided for special protection of the rights of all three religions in Jerusalem, but the first real attempt to come to grips with the realities of Palestine was the British Royal Commission Report of 1936-37, better known as the report of the Peel Commission. The commission recommended that Palestine be partitioned into an Arab state and a Jewish state and that there be created "a British Enclave, under permanent Mandate, which would include Jerusalem and Bethlehem for reasons of Christian tradition and Lydda and Ramleh and a corridor to the sea at Jaffa for military and economic reasons." [3] Nearly ten years later the Morrison-Grady Plan, devised to implement the recommendations of the 1946 Anglo-American Committee on Palestine, also postulated the need for continued British control over Jerusalem and its Holy Places.[4] But it proved impossible for Britain to create a stable situation in Palestine or reconcile conflicting and contradictory claims, and the problem of the future of Palestine and Jerusalem was handed over to the United Nations.

In view of the international community's concern over Jerusalem, it was hardly surprising that the United Nations Special Committee on Palestine (UNSCOP), created by the General Assembly to recommend a policy for the future of Palestine, proposed that Jerusalem be internationalized. This was seen as the best way to protect the rights and interests of all three religions in their common Holy City. UNSCOP's study resulted in the partition plan incorporated in the General Assembly's Resolution 181 of November 29, 1947, adopted with the support of the Soviet Union as well as the United States, but opposed by the Arab states. (Israel, of course, was not a member of the United Nations at that time.) Under Part III of this resolution Jerusalem was to have the status of a *corpus separatum* ("separate entity") under a special international regime to be administered by the United Nations Trusteeship Council. The area was to include the city of Jerusalem

---

[2] Text in J. C. Hurewitz, *Diplomacy in the Near and Middle East,* vol. I (Princeton, 1956), pp. 153-56.

[3] *Palestine: A Study of Jewish, Arab and British Policies* (published for the Esco Foundation for Palestine, New Haven: Yale University Press, 1947), p. 846.

[4] Fred J. Khouri, *The Arab-Israeli Dilemma* (Syracuse: Syracuse University Press, 1968), p. 102.

itself as well as a region including certain neighboring villages and towns, the southernmost being Bethlehem. A governor was to be appointed by and responsible to the Trusteeship Council; he was to exercise all powers of administration including the conduct of foreign affairs. There were provisions for the special protection of the Holy Places, and Jerusalem was to be demilitarized and neutralized, with no military or paramilitary activities permitted within its borders.[5] The plan was never implemented. A final vote on the draft statute (T. 188/Rev. 2) of the Trusteeship Council was postponed by the convocation of a special session of the General Assembly to review the entire Palestine problem. With the British mandate coming to an end in May 1948 and with the increase of violence in the area, the trusteeship plan was set aside.

Plans for the internationalization of Jerusalem met with opposition from the Jewish Agency (and later at times from Israel); the Arab states generally were also opposed. The Jewish Agency proposed a sort of quasi-internationalization: "an international regime which applied to the whole city, but which is restricted functionally so as to be concerned only with the protection and control of the Holy Places and not with any purely secular or political aspects of life and government."[6] The Vatican and many of the Roman Catholic countries of Latin America, now joined by the Arab states (except Jordan), countered with a renewal of the idea of territorial internationalization, a *corpus separatum* covering a territory about the size of the area envisaged under General Assembly Resolution 181.[7]

During the Palestinian war of 1948, Israel occupied the new section of Jerusalem, while Transjordan occupied the old city with almost all of the Holy Places. The armistice agreement of 1949 between Transjordan and Israel merely confirmed the de facto military situation along Israel's eastern front; it made no reference to internationalization of Jerusalem.[8] The Arabs now held the Gaza Strip and the West Bank of the Jordan, including East Jerusalem. At least two important groups of Palestinians met about this time to discuss the future of Palestine. On the West Bank, the Jericho Congress was convened on December 1, 1948, under the auspices of King Abdullah of Transjordan. Over 2,000 delegates from all parts of Palestine attended; many were elected officials, *mukhtars,* tribal chiefs and mayors. In their seven-point resolution the delegates proclaimed Abdullah king of all Palestine.[9] In effect, the Congress through its delegates turned over the sovereignty of the West Bank and East Jerusalem to the king — whose army, in fact, occupied the territories in question. The British government endorsed the resolutions of the Jericho Congress. It has been argued that Israel,

[5] For text of Resolution 181 of November 29, 1947, see *Year Book of the United Nations, 1947-48* (published by the Department of Public Information of the United Nations), pp. 247-57. Hereinafter cited as *UN Year Book* and year. See also references in Chapter II, note 11; see also Ralph H. Magnus, ed., *Documents on the Middle East* (Washington: American Enterprise Institute for Public Policy Research, 1969), pp. 144-60.

[6] Abba Eban before the Ad Hoc Political Committee, as reported in *The Peace of Jerusalem* (Jerusalem: Israel Office of Information, 1949).

[7] Edward B. Glick, "The Vatican, Latin America and Jerusalem," *International Organization,* vol. II (Spring 1957), pp. 217ff.

[8] Text of the armistice agreement in *United Nations Treaty Series,* vol. 49 (1949), pp. 304-25.

[9] Aqil Hyder Hasan Abidi, *Jordan: A Political Study, 1948-1957* (Bombay: Asia Publishing House, 1965), p. 54.

with the signing of the Israel-Jordan armistice agreement, tacitly ratified the union of the West Bank and East Jerusalem with Transjordan (later Jordan). Others have maintained that this "union" was simply annexation: it followed the conquest of these areas by the Transjordanian army, the Arab Legion; the mandated territory of Palestine had ceased to exist. Whatever the merits of these positions, it is nevertheless indisputable that the Jericho Congress produced a consensus among an impressive number of important Palestinian leaders: they, as much as anyone else, could claim representation of the Palestinian people — at least those of the West Bank.

Meanwhile, with Egyptian support and for reasons largely reflecting divisions in inter-Arab politics, an all-Palestinian government was formed in the Gaza Strip, physically separated from the West Bank by the armistice lines. It claimed to represent all of Palestine, including those portions "occupied by Israel," and it denounced the resolutions of the Jericho Congress.[10] This group has represented Palestine in the Arab League since 1949. Arab Palestinian leadership has never been conspicuous for its unity, but the lack of unity displayed at the time of the Jericho Congress and the establishment of the Gaza government was probably in part a function of the geographical separation between the two groups imposed by the armistice lines.

General Assembly Resolution 181, adopting the partition plan, called for the election by the assembly of a five-man commission, with international representation from states not directly involved, to which the administration of Palestine was to be progressively turned over as British troops withdrew. When the 1948 fighting was over, the commission was instructed by the General Assembly to produce a detailed proposal for a permanent international regime for the Jerusalem area.[11] After consulting the parties most directly concerned, the commission recommended that Jerusalem be divided into two sections, one to be administered by Israel and the other by Jordan, while an international administration under the United Nations would control the Holy Places, supervise demilitarization, and protect human rights.[12]

The positions of both Israel and Jordan on Jerusalem changed after the Arab-Israel war of 1948. Israel, which had once been willing, albeit reluctantly, to accept the partition resolution, was now in possession of the greater part of Jerusalem. Israel now opposed any form of internationalization, asserting that it would be responsible for Jewish Jerusalem, its 100,000 Jewish inhabitants, and the Holy Places. Most Arab governments now concluded that it would be in the Arab interest to internationalize the city, but King Abdullah insisted that Jordan itself could safeguard the old part of the city and the majority of the Holy Places. Israel incorporated the portion of Jerusalem controlled by its forces, and on February 14, 1949, President Chaim Weizmann opened the first session of the Israeli

---

[10] Ibid., p. 56.

[11] General Assembly Resolution 194 (III), December 11, 1948; text in *UN Year Book, 1948-1949*, pp. 174-76; see also Magnus, *Documents on the Middle East*, pp. 161-63.

[12] Pablo de Azcarate, *Mission in Palestine, 1948-1952* (Washington: Middle East Institute, 1966), pp. 181-88.

Constituent Assembly, or Knesset, in Jerusalem.[13] Despite formal disapproval by the United Nations, Israel proclaimed Jerusalem as its capital and moved many government offices there.[14] By 1949, then, one portion of Jerusalem was considered by Israel as its capital, and the other portion had become Jordan's second largest city—a city of considerable strategic, political, economic and religious importance.

The international community repeatedly expressed its dissatisfaction over this situation. In both the fourth and fifth sessions of the General Assembly of the United Nations, in 1949 and 1950, the subject of Jerusalem was debated at length.[15] But the more the international community talked of internationalization, the more adamant became Prime Minister Ben Gurion and King Abdullah in asserting their rights to their respective portions. Although the *corpus separatum* resolutions and the condemnations of Israel's actions regarding Jerusalem were still legally in force as far as the United Nations was concerned, and although some 30 states kept their embassies in Tel Aviv by way of protest, little could be done to change the practical situation. Both countries incorporated provisions in their domestic legislation for the protection and maintenance of the holy sites. Between 1953 and 1967 Jerusalem was discussed only rarely at the United Nations; both Israel and Jordan seemed to find the situation tolerable. If Israel had any idea of incorporating the old city or the West Bank, it did not surface in 1956, when quiet reigned along the Israel-Jordan border throughout the Sinai campaign. Up to 1967, then, the legal formulations of the international community through the United Nations were being disregarded in the face of the political realities of the divided land and the divided city.

Since the June War of 1967, in the absence of a peace settlement, Israel has deemed it necessary, as the occupying power, to introduce many measures reflecting its assumption of administrative duties formerly undertaken by the governments whose territory is now under occupation. With respect to Jerusalem, Israel has gone much further. The conquest of Jerusalem evoked a tremendous emotional response from Israelis and Jews everywhere: for Jerusalem was at last united and Israel was now in possession of the Wailing Wall, which had effectively been denied to Jews since 1948. On June 9, 1967, even before the war was over, the municipal authorities of the Israeli sector of Jerusalem approved a fund of 150 million Israeli pounds to restore and rebuild "united Jerusalem." [16] On June 15 the water systems and power grids of the two sectors were joined, and joint administrative services such as the transportation system were established.[17] The government purported to legalize its *fait accompli* in three laws passed by the Knesset on June 27.[18] The first of these amended the Law and Administration Ordinance to provide that the law, jurisdiction, and administration of Israel should apply in any

[13] Oscar Kraines, *Israel: The Emergence of a New Nation* (Washington: Public Affairs Press, 1954), p. 8.

[14] *UN Year Book, 1948-49*, pp. 196-97.

[15] Ibid., pp. 190-97; also *UN Year Book, 1949-50*, pp. 337-41.

[16] *Jerusalem Post,* June 9, 1967.

[17] *New York Times,* June 28, 1967.

[18] "Declaration of the Extension of the Boundaries of the Jerusalem Corporation," *Israeli Government Official Gazette,* June 28, 1967.

area of "Eretz Israel" as designated by the government. The second amended the Municipal Corporations Ordinance of 1934 to permit the minister of interior to enlarge by proclamation the area of Jerusalem's municipal corporation to include any area designated under the Law and Administration Ordinance. The third measure provided for the protection of the Holy Places and for freedom of access to them. The next day the minister of interior proceeded to designate as part of Jerusalem (pursuant to the amended Law and Administration Ordinance) the former Jordanian sector and surrounding territory including Kallandiyya Airport, the Mount of Olives, Mount Scopus, and several villages.

On July 4, 1967, the United Nations General Assembly voted to declare the unification of Jerusalem invalid; it called upon Israel to "rescind all measures already taken and to desist forthwith from taking any action which would alter the status of Jerusalem." [19] Israel has taken no action in response to this directive.

The Occupied Territories in International Law

The present situation in Jerusalem, the West Bank, the Gaza Strip, the Golan Heights, and the Sinai Peninsula requires consideration of the precepts of international law relating to belligerent occupation. The need to create rules to protect the rights of civilians in time of war has only been recognized in the twentieth century. As Professor McDougal has pointed out, legal principles or codes that have been developed to deal with such problems reflect the need for a balance between humanitarianism and military necessity.[20] The two principal international conventions bearing on this subject, the Hague Regulations of 1907 [21] and the Geneva Convention of 1949,[22] emphasize above all the necessity of maintaining the "vie publique." In other words, the main concern is that the war situation and occupation by an enemy power should disrupt civilian life ("vie publique") as little as possible.[23]

The standard definition of occupation has been stated by Oppenheim:

> . . . invasion plus the taking possession of an enemy country for the purpose of holding it, at any rate temporarily. The difference between mere invasion and occupation becomes apparent from the fact that an occupant sets up some kind of administration, whereas the mere invader does not.[24]

Occupation does not displace or transfer sovereignty. The occupant may exercise

---

[19] General Assembly Resolution 2253 (ES-V); see also Magnus, *Documents on the Middle East*, p. 203.

[20] Myres S. McDougal and Florentino P. Feliciano, *Law and Minimum World Public Order: The Legal Regulation of International Coercion* (New Haven: Yale University Press, 1960), p. 75.

[21] James Brown Scott, ed., *The Hague Conventions and Declarations of 1899 and 1907*, "Section III: Military Authority over the Territory of the Hostile State," (New York: Oxford University Press, 1915), pp. 122-27.

[22] *The Geneva Conventions Relative to the Protection of Civilian Persons in Time of War*, August 12, 1949 (Dept. of State Publication 3938, August 1950), pp. 164-216. Text also appears in *American Journal of International Law*, vol. 50 (1956), pp. 724-77.

[23] McDougal and Feliciano, *Law and Minimum World Public Order*, p. 746.

[24] Cited in Lord McNair and A. D. Watts, *The Legal Effects of War* (Cambridge University Press, 1966), pp. 367-68.

military authority, but does not acquire sovereignty unless or until it is ceded to the occupant by treaty of peace, or is abandoned in its favor without cession, or is acquired by virtue of subjugation—that is, by elimination of the local sovereign and annexation of the latter's territory.[25]

There is no question that annexation of occupied territory is illegal under international law. It may be noted that with regard to Jerusalem, Israel avoided the term "annexation" in favor of "administrative union," though the validity of any distinction based on such terminology is questionable, inasmuch as all administrative functions have been assumed by Israel, Israeli currency is used, and Israeli civil law applies. Most significantly, Israel has declared this "administrative union" to be "irrevocable." [26]

While such measures in lieu of formal annexation are legally questionable, there are precedents for such measures in recent history. For instance, Belgium in World War I and Poland in World War II were divided by the Germans into separate administrative and political units. As Draper has pointed out, these measures "had the effect of moving certain occupied areas outside the regime of the Hague Regulations of 1907, and, in effect, permitting the occupant to set up his own unfettered type of administration." Draper notes that the Hague Regulations were so uncertain and lacking in detail as to permit evasion: "There were devices such as premature annexation during war, whereby the occupant sought to avoid the obligations, such as they were, in the Hague Regulations, and to convert his limited authority into that of sovereignty." [27]

In considering the legality or illegality of Israel's "administrative union" with respect to Jerusalem, it is necessary to take into account the concept of state sovereignty, or the "act of state" doctrine, as it is known in international law. In purporting to absorb Jerusalem by administrative union, Israel went through the necessary legal procedures as far as Israel's own law is concerned. As mentioned above, an enabling act was passed authorizing the minister of interior to incorporate new territory into the municipality. The following day he did so. Similarly, he was authorized by Israeli legislation to extend Jerusalem's boundaries to accommodate immigrants, and in January 1968 he exercised that authority.[28] It might be difficult to challenge such actions in an Israeli court, for, as Felix Morgenstern has pointed out, "acts done in connection with the annexation of foreign territory are in some countries regarded as acts of state and cannot be reviewed by the courts." [29]

But leaving aside Israeli jurisprudence for the moment, what about the "act of state" doctrine as applied in other forums? The doctrine was stated by the United States Supreme Court in 1897 in the leading case of *Underhill* v. *Hernandez* (168 U.S. 250) as follows: "Every sovereign state is bound to respect the independence of every other sovereign state, and the courts of one country will not sit in

25 Ibid., pp. 368-69.

26 Abba Eban, quoted in *New York Times*, July 14, 1967.

27 G. I. A. D. Draper, "The Geneva Conventions of 1949," *Recueil Des Cours: 1965-I,* vol. 114 (Leyden, 1965), p. 121.

28 *New York Times,* January 12, 1968.

29Felix Morgenstern, "Judicial Practice and the Supremacy of International Law," *British Year Book of International Law,* vol. 27 (1950), p. 75.

judgment on the acts of the government of another *done within its own territory."*
(Emphasis supplied.) Jerusalem, of course, was not in Israeli territory at the time
the enabling act was passed; consequently, it seems likely that a tribunal following
the rule of *Underhill* v. *Hernandez* would have considerable difficulty in recognizing the applicability of the act of state doctrine as far as the Jerusalem situation
is concerned.

Israel's legislation on Jerusalem raises other questions. Did the well-established
international legal principles relating to belligerent occupation apply only until
June 28, the day when the laws were implemented? Or, assuming these actions
tantamount to annexation are prima facie prohibited by international law, and at
all events were condemned by the world community through the United Nations,[30] must "East Jerusalem" still be regarded as occupied territory? No
tribunal has yet been asked to rule on these points, but the Geneva Convention of
1949 (Article 47) would appear to apply to at least a part of the problem:

> Protected persons who are in occupied territory shall not be deprived, in
> any case or in any manner whatsoever, of the benefits of the present
> Convention by any change introduced, as the result of the occupation of
> a territory, into the institutions or government of the said territory, nor
> by any agreement concluded between the authorities of the occupied
> territories and the Occupying Power, nor by any annexation by the
> latter of the whole or part of the occupied territory.

In other words, the benefits afforded by the convention cannot be infringed by
actions of any of the types enumerated, and the niceties of terminology would
appear to be of little consequence, at least in this context. (The Geneva Convention is considered in more detail below.)

International law principles relating to belligerent occupation clearly apply to
the occupied areas whose status, unlike that of Jerusalem, Israel has not purported
to change. In terms of practical politics and Israel's military situation, there are
differences among these areas: Golan and Sinai are strategically important yet
sparsely populated, while Gaza and the West Bank have large Arab populations
whose absorption under an Israeli regime would undoubtedly prove trou-
blesome.[31] But from the standpoint of Israel's legal obligations as an occupying
power, the problems and questions are substantially identical for all four areas.
For administrative purposes Israel has divided these territories into four regions:
the West Bank of the Jordan (called "Judea and Samaria"); the Gaza Strip and
Northern Sinai; the Golan District; and Southern Sinai ("Solomon Area").[32]
Four different legal systems still apply in these territories: Jordanian law in the
West Bank; Egyptian in Sinai; Syrian in Golan; and Palestinian, as modified by

---

[30] General Assembly Resolutions 2253 (ES-V) and 2254 (ES-V), reprinted in *UN Monthly
Chronicle,* July 1967, p. 77, and August-September 1967, p. 20, respectively; see also Magnus,
Documents on the Middle East, p. 203.

[31] Nadav Safran, *From War to War: The Arab-Israeli Confrontation 1948-1967* (New
York: Pegasus, 1969), p. 407. There are some 400,000 Arabs in Gaza and nearly a million
on the West Bank. About 7,000, mostly Druzes, remain in the Golan Heights. Sinai contains
about 100,000 Arabs, most of them near al-Arish on the Mediterranean, some moved there
from the Suez Canal area. For Gaza, see *New York Times,* April 22, 1969.

[32] Nimrod Raphaeli, "Military Government in the Occupied Territories: An Israeli View,"
Middle East Journal, vol. 23, no. 2 (Spring 1969), pp. 177-90.

the Gaza Ordinance of 1958, in the Gaza Strip.[33] (Some Israelis have called for their replacement by Israeli Laws.)[34]

Article 56 of the Hague Regulations of 1907 deals with the treatment of private and municipal property:

> The property of municipalities, that of institutions dedicated to religion, charity, and education, the arts and sciences, even when state property, shall be treated as private property. All seizure of, destruction or willful damage done to institutions of this character, historic monuments, works of art and science is forbidden and should be made the subject of legal proceedings.

Similarly, Article 53 of the Geneva Convention provides:

> Any destruction by the Occupying Power of real or personal property belonging individually or collectively to private persons, or to the State, or to other public authorities, or to social or cooperative organizations is prohibited, except where such destruction is rendered absolutely necessary by military operations.

Several of the municipal buildings in the Jordanian sector of Jerusalem have been taken over for use as Israeli government offices. Israeli police headquarters, for example, have been moved to the Old City. Many private houses were razed, especially near the Wailing Wall, in order to accommodate the numerous pilgrims wishing to pray there. Israeli authorities have stated that alternate housing was offered for the displaced inhabitants, in accordance with Article 49 of the Geneva Convention: "The Occupying Power undertaking such transfers or evacuations shall insure, to the greatest practicable extent, that proper accommodation is provided to receive the protected persons. . . ." Some doubt, however, has been expressed as to whether such an offer was genuinely made, and in any case none of the displaced persons are believed to have taken advantage of it. Jerusalem's Mayor Teddy Kollek conceded in 1968 that "some Arab families were removed from their homes at too short notice and without replacement housing for them having first been found." [35]

With a steady increase in Arab guerrilla activity after June 1967, the Israeli government resorted to dynamiting houses thought to be sheltering rebels. These measures went largely unreported until March 1968, when Mayor Kollek publicly rebuked the military for blowing up a house in Jerusalem.[36] On another occasion Arab shops were seized by Israeli authorities in Jerusalem after a strike of Arab merchants.[37] Arabs elsewhere also faced destruction of their property in the wake of terrorist activities and resistance to Israeli authorities;[38] Nablus, site

---

[33] When Egypt re-entered the Gaza Strip following Israeli evacuation after the 1956 Suez war, laws were passed giving Palestinians there a greater voice in local affairs. *New York Times,* March 12 and 16, 1958.

[34] *New York Times,* March 5 and April 7, 1969. Moshe Dayan, in a speech, urged specifically that Israeli laws be applied to the West Bank. At the same time he urged that Israel bar "any movement of Arab population from the occupied territories into Israel and any attempt by Arabs in those areas to become Israeli citizens."

[35] *Washington Post,* May 2, 1968, p. A 23.

[36] *Washington Post,* April 7, 1968, p. B 7.

[37] *New York Times,* November 3, 1968.

[38] *Christian Science Monitor,* April 30, 1969.

of a large West Bank refugee camp and an Arab prison, and Gaza were scenes of frequent tension and violence; [39] the authorities had to deal with acts such as bombings at a bus terminal, a marketplace, and the Hebrew University.[40] In this sort of environment it is not easy to sort out the equities, but the Geneva Convention sets definite standards (Article 33): "No protected person may be punished for an offence he or she has not personally committed. Collective penalties and likewise all measures of intimidation or of terrorism are prohibited. Reprisals against protected persons and their property are prohibited." Article 53 of the Hague Regulations provides that "communication and transportation facilities, even private, may be taken, but must be restored when peace is made." This provision will have to be taken into account in connection with the eventual return of Kallandiyya Airport which, as mentioned above, has now been incorporated into the expanded boundaries of Jerusalem pursuant to measures taken by the Israelis which they have declared to be "irrevocable."

The evacuation of hundreds of people from the area near the Wailing Wall in 1967 has to be viewed in the light of Article 49 of the Geneva Convention:

> Individual or mass forcible transfers, as well as deportations of protected persons from occupied territory to the territory of the Occupying Power or to that of any other country, occupied or not, are prohibited, regardless of their motive.
>
> Nevertheless, the Occupying Power may undertake total or partial evacuation of a given area *if the security of the population or imperative military reasons so demand.* . . . Persons thus evacuated shall be transferred back to their homes as soon as hostilities in the area in question have ceased. (Emphasis supplied.)

As far as is known, no security or military reasons were advanced for clearing the residential area near the Wailing Wall and evacuating the inhabitants.

When certain religious and political leaders were deported in the autumn of 1967, the deportation was justified not on the grounds specified in Article 49, but rather on an emergency regulation of the British dating back to 1945 but kept in force by Israel, authorizing the deportation of dangerous persons.[41]

Protests, often involving violence, in occupied territory have sometimes been dealt with in a manner that appears to be at variance with the international canons established with regard to belligerent occupation. It must be borne in mind, however, that from the Israeli standpoint violent demonstrations aggravate an already tense security situation, especially in such sensitive and heavily populated areas as the Gaza Strip and the West Bank. Arab women, especially in Gaza, have at times led the resistance to Israeli rule; riots and demonstrations have resulted in deaths and many injuries as the authorities moved quickly to restore order.[42] Arabs on the West Bank have frequently demonstrated in

---

[39] *Christian Science Monitor,* April 4, 1969. Regarding the prison, see *New York Times,* September 6, 1968.

[40] *New York Times,* September 7, 1968, November 23, 1968, and March 16, 1969.

[41] *New York Times,* January 2, 1968.

[42] *New York Times,* February 2, 1969 and April 22, 1969. *Washington Post,* April 12, 1969, p. F 1.

support of their compatriots in Gaza.[43] While the killing in Gaza of an Arab magistrate in 1968 was presumably unlawful,[44] and while other similar incidents have taken place, the Israelis in general have tried to act within existing laws. As the occupying power, however, they appear to have adopted a somewhat uncompromising concept of security: strikes and other essentially peaceful demonstrations are treated with severity. Travel curbs on Arabs in all of the occupied territories have been used to quell resistance;[45] from the Arab standpoint such measures appear tantamount to economic strangulation.

Muslim religious leaders have registered complaints arising from the application of Israeli laws and regulations.[46] Article 27 of the Geneva Convention provides: "Protected persons are entitled, in all circumstances, to respect for their persons, their honour, their family rights, their religious convictions and practices, and their manners and customs." In 1967 the Mufti of Jerusalem lodged a complaint concerning the curtailment of Muslim religious rights in all occupied territories. He contended that he was allowed to hold services only once a week, while Muslims were accustomed to visit the mosque much more frequently.[47] On the other hand, Israel has taken steps to cooperate with various religious groups. About a year after the June war, Israel quietly agreed to help three church groups repair property damaged in the war. On another occasion Mayor Kollek, despite opposition in the Knesset, approved Muslim plans to build memorials in Jerusalem to Arabs killed in action.[48]

Complaints have also been registered on behalf of various professional groups. Article 52 of the Geneva Convention prohibits "all measures aiming at creating unemployment or at restricting the opportunities offered to workers in an occupied territory"; and Article 54 provides that "the Occupying Power may not alter the status of public officials or judges. . . ." After the "administrative union" of Jerusalem, all professionals, including doctors and lawyers, were required to have Israeli licenses. Lawyers and judges were required to use Hebrew. While such regulations were presumably adopted as a matter of administrative convenience, they have nevertheless had the practical effect of seriously inhibiting the opportunities for a significant element of the educated Arab population to pursue their professions.[49]

Increased immigration to Israel, called for by government officials after the June war, gave rise to still another issue. In January 1968, some 838 acres of occupied territory outside Jerusalem's city limits were expropriated to accommodate Jewish settlers, and construction of a housing development was begun on the property.[50] According to Article 49 of the Geneva Convention, the occupying power is not permitted to "transfer part of its own civilian population into the

---

[43] For example, see *New York Times,* January 28, 1969.

[44] *New York Times,* September 17, 1968.

[45] *New York Times,* December 8, 1968.

[46] Report by Secretary-General U Thant, *UN Monthly Chronicle,* October 1967, p. 12.

[47] *New York Times,* June 28, 1967.

[48] *New York Times,* June 2 and December 20, 1968.

[49] A similar law that would bring all Arab business in Jerusalem under Israeli laws and regulations has been contemplated. *Washington Post,* February 10, 1969; *New York Times,* April 28, 1969.

[50] *New York Times,* January 12, 1968; *Washington Post,* February 24, 1968.

territory it occupies." Israel could point out that it had not actually transferred its population, but had simply invited immigrants to the newly acquired territory; the distinction would be challenged by many jurists on the basis of the maintenance of the "vie publique," which—as pointed out above—lies at the core of the international principles relating to belligerent occupation. Legal technicalities aside, the episode has created much resentment among the Arabs.

A nagging question remains. Just how effective are the rules of international law relating to belligerent occupation when applied to a specific situation? Many practical problems are bound to arise, and Article 53 of the Geneva Convention provides a good illustration: "Any destruction by the Occupying Power of real or personal property . . . is prohibited, *except where such destruction is rendered absolutely necessary by military operations.*" A justification based on military necessity is easy to claim, harder to disprove. In general, courts have tended to be reluctant to examine actions justified as safeguards of public order.[51] Moreover, what tribunal would entertain a challenge to the legality of measures undertaken by Israel in the occupied territories? Professor Quincy Wright has urged: ". . . doubtless there are definite rules of International Law limiting the authority of a military occupant during the course of the war. Acts of such de facto authority which ignore these limitations, even though functioning locally, should be regarded as *ultra vires* and void by a foreign court." [52]

Felix Morgenstern agrees that "such acts should be treated as a legal nullity both by the courts of the occupied country during the occupation—where they have the power to do so—and by the returning sovereign." He adds the following caution:

> In its practical application, however, certain limitations on that principle must be noted. In the first instance, too sweeping an interpretation must not be given to the phrase 'unlawful acts of the occupant.' While municipal courts during the occupation have affirmed that they will not enforce measures of the Occupant which go beyond the powers permitted him by international law, they have been reluctant to inquire whether legislative measures which *prima facie* could be intended to safeguard public order, and thus to satisfy the requirements of Article 43 of the Hague Regulations [analogous to Article 53 of the Geneva Convention], were in fact necessary.[53]

The authority and competence of Arab judges in the occupied territories is severely circumscribed. Israeli courts, of course, have jurisdiction to rule upon the validity of their government's actions, and it is possible that such rulings might be made despite the tense political environment. Foreign courts, as far as is known, have not yet had occasion to examine the legality of such aspects of the Israeli occupation as have been outlined above. Finally, there is the possibility that the "returning sovereign" may eventually return, as suggested by Morgenstern, to exercise the appropriate jurisdiction. In the meantime, the effective lack of legal

---

[51] Felix Morgenstern, "Validity of the Acts of the Belligerent Occupant," *British Year Book of International Law,* vol. 28 (1951), p. 306.

[52] Quincy Wright, "Editorial Comment," *American Journal of International Law,* vol. 31 (1937), p. 687n.

[53] Morgenstern, "Belligerent Occupant," *supra,* note 51, pp. 300, 305-06.

channels for the adjudication of grievances provides a frustration for the Arabs of Jerusalem and the other occupied territories. In the circumstances, protest by violence would appear to be predictable.

There remains the United Nations. The Arab states have repeatedly brought matters relating to the occupied territories to the attention of the United Nations Human Rights Commission. In 1969 the commission passed a resolution providing for the establishment of a "special committee to investigate Israeli practices affecting the human rights of the population of territories occupied as a result of the June 1967 War." [54] The special committee, composed of representatives of Ceylon, Somalia and Yugoslavia, has been conducting a series of investigations in Arab countries, interviewing many refugees who fled from the Occupied Territories. However, because of Israeli objections to the committee's composition and the nature of its mandate, it was not given access to the Occupied Territories. Its preliminary report, submitted to the General Assembly in October 1970, stated that the human rights of Arabs in the Occupied Territories had been violated.[55] This report relied heavily upon the well established principles of international law relating to belligerent occupation, as codified in the Hague Regulations of 1907 and the Geneva Convention of 1949.

Claims Relating to Jerusalem and the Occupied Territories

As noted above, both Israel and Jordan have well-developed positions based on historical and present claims to rights in Palestine. But these states are not the only entities with claims relating to the Holy Land and the occupied territories generally. Egypt has claims on the Sinai Peninsula and, to a lesser extent, the Gaza Strip; Syria's claim to the Golan Heights is just as strong as Egypt's in Sinai. There are increasingly articulate claims on behalf of the Palestinians themselves. And finally, the international community at large can be said to have rights in Palestine, especially Jerusalem.

Israeli Claims. Israel's claims to Palestine on the basis of prior possession in ancient times need not be developed here—not because Israelis have not asserted such claims, but rather because Israel has more persuasive arguments. The basic document is the Balfour Declaration of 1917. The Peel Commission Report (1937) and the United Nations partition plan (1947) confirmed widespread international support for the establishment of a Jewish homeland. In the face of Arab protests that Palestine was not Britain's to give away, that Palestinians had been denied the right of self-determination, that the inhabitants opposed the partition plan, and that the world community could not force such a solution, by 1947-48 the majority of the international community appeared to support the establishment of Israel as a Jewish state.

After the Palestinian war of 1948 and the armistice agreement of 1949, Israel and Jordan shared in the dismemberment of Jerusalem. Both ignored international

---

[54] *UN Monthly Chronicle,* January 1969, p. 124.
[55] UN General Assembly Document A/8089, October 1970; see also *UN Monthly Chronicle,* May 1971, pp. 50-87.

protest implemented in several United Nations resolutions asserting Jerusalem's international status.

Israel's position after the June war was set forth by Prime Minister Levi Eshkol in a statement on October 30, 1967:

> The area that was under Jordanian occupation . . . and the Gaza Region which the Egyptians ruled were held by them not by right but by force, as the result of military aggression and occupation. This occupation was recognized, it is true, in the armistice agreements . . . but these agreements have been nullified by military provocation and aggression on their part.[56]

It has been argued that "the sovereignty vacuum arising in the Old City [and perhaps the West Bank] at the end of the Mandate was not filled by Jordan, whose status there was one of *de facto* occupation protected by the Armistice Agreement." Thus in 1967, "once Jordan was physically removed from the Old City by legitimate measures—as the Israeli reactions to the Jordanian attack on June 5, 1967, undoubtedly were—then the way was open for a lawful occupant to fill the still subsisting vacancy." [57]

Israel has also justified its incorporation of East Jerusalem in 1967 on the ground that Jordan had violated the 1949 armistice agreement by refusing Jews access to the Wailing Wall. Israelis point to the fact that the international community acquiesced for many years in Jordan's unilateral control over the Holy Places in the Old City; it should not now fear unilateral Israeli control. "International interest in Jerusalem," declared Prime Minister Eshkol in 1967, "has always been understood to derive from the presence of the Holy Places. Israel has the will and the capacity to secure respect for the universal spiritual interests." Eshkol continued:

> The term "annexation" used by the supporters of the July 1967 UN Resolution condemning Israeli action taken to change Jerusalem's status is out of place. . . . The measures adopted relate to the integration of Jerusalem in the administrative and municipal spheres and furnish a legal basis for the protection of the Holy Places in Jerusalem.[58]

In response to the July 1967 resolutions of the United Nations condemning Israel's actions, the Prime Minister said:

> . . . a salient fact of Jerusalem's life is the necessity of insuring equal rights and opportunities to all the city's residents by extending to them the same public services and facilities. No international or other interest would be served by instituting divisions and barriers which would only sharpen tensions and generate discrimination.[59]

Many Israelis feel that if Syria and Egypt continue to refuse to negotiate peace, Israel should annex Sinai and the Golan Heights.[60] It is argued that Egypt's

---

[56] *New York Times,* October 31, 1967.
[57] Elihu Lauterpacht, *Jerusalem and the Holy Places* (London: The Anglo-Israel Association, 1968), p. 48.
[58] *New York Times,* July 14, 1967.
[59] *UN Monthly Chronicle,* October 1967, p. 13.
[60] Safran, *From War to War,* p. 407.

position in Sinai is relatively recent; its expanded presence there came with British help in 1892 and 1907. In ancient times, moreover, Sinai was important to the Jews. "Both [Egypt and Israel]," it has been asserted, "have possessed whole or part of it at various periods of history. But when the reckoning comes, Israel's claims may prove to be far more enduring than Egypt's." [61]

Jordanian Claims. Since 1967 Jordan has resorted less than formerly to the argument heard so frequently during the discussions of partition in the late 1940s— that Palestine was not Britain's to give away. Basically, the Jordanians now urge a return to the status established by the 1949 armistice agreement. They contend that annexation by Israel of any of the occupied territories is illegal on the basis of United Nations resolutions and international law generally. Brushing aside the charge that denying access of Jews to the Wailing Wall was a violation of the armistice agreement, they point to Israel's activities in the Mount Scopus area. This area was an enclave inside Jordanian-administered territory from 1949 to 1967. While it was supposedly under United Nations jurisdiction, Israel in fact controlled Mount Scopus and would not permit United Nations inspection of the area; it had been widely reported that the Israelis had cached arms there, in contravention of Jerusalem's demilitarized status. Jordan maintains that it managed the Holy Places well, consulted with leaders of religious groups involved (not, however, Jewish groups), and also incorporated a "Protection of the Holy Places" provision in its laws, as Israel also did shortly after the June war.[62]

In reply to Israel's allegation that Jordan illegally occupied Jerusalem and the West Bank, Jordan has referred to the resolution adopted at the Jericho Congress in December 1948, mentioned above, and to the armistice agreement of 1949. Jordan points out that the union of the West Bank and Jerusalem with Transjordan was ratified by the Transjordan cabinet on December 13, 1948, and contends that Britain and the United States recognized it within a month.

Palestinian Claims. The claims of Palestinian leaders have not been well-articulated until recently; nor have the Palestinian people themselves been united behind a single spokesman. As noted above, from 1948 on there were at least two groups claiming to represent Palestinian Arabs: those present at the Jericho Congress who accepted Jordan's sovereignty over the West Bank, and the all-Palestinian government formed in Gaza, which later moved to Cairo (where it remained relatively inactive). After the June war the Palestinian refugees became more and more vocal in the political sense; leaders among the guerrillas began to speak for all Palestinians. The guerrillas, while not completely united, represent a force with claims to Palestine which must inevitably be heard if there is to be a settlement of the Arab-Israeli conflict. Many Palestinians assert a legal claim to all of Palestine, maintaining that the only just solution would be the creation of a state in which Jews and Arabs could live as equals and as Palestinians.[63]

Syrian and Egyptian Claims. Syria and Egypt would appear to have unquestion-

---

[61] Sidney Sugarman, quoted in *The Christian Science Monitor,* April 18, 1969, from *The Jewish Observer and Middle East Review* (London, April 1969).

[62] Lauterpacht, *Jerusalem and the Holy Places,* p. 55.

[63] See, for example, *Look Magazine,* May 13, 1969.

ably valid claims for the return of the Golan Heights and Sinai, respectively, inasmuch as these territories lie within their internationally recognized borders. They deny that Israel has any right to occupy or annex any part of them, and they reject any justification based on Israeli security considerations. Since Israel refuses to withdraw on security grounds until Syria and Egypt make peace, the concept of "security and peace" from the Israeli standpoint is clearly an important factor in the resolution of this territorial problem.[64]

In addition to assertions of a right and a duty to defend Arab rights in Palestine, Egypt maintains a claim to the Gaza Strip based on its former legal position there. From 1948 to 1967, except briefly during the 1956 Suez war, Egypt had administrative control over the Strip, although the United Nations Emergency Force patrolled its borders adjoining Israel from 1956 to 1967. It is perhaps significant, however, that while complaining of the treatment of Arabs in Israeli-occupied Gaza, Egypt has apparently not adopted a strong or precise position on the future status of the Strip—which, after all, is part of Palestine, not Egypt. Nor has Israel shown as great an interest in this area as in other parts of the occupied territories where refugees are not so densely concentrated.

Third Party "Claims." Others besides the principal disputants have shown a deep interest and concern for a resolution of the Arab-Israeli dilemma, and thus may be said to have claims of their own. Among them are religious groups, notably Catholics represented by the Vatican and Eastern Churches represented by their patriarchs, who have a long and deep involvement in Palestine and especially in Jerusalem. In view of the focus of so many religious interests in the Holy Land, and because of its fundamental responsibilities for the maintenance of peace, the United Nations has been deeply involved in Palestine almost since its inception at the end of World War II. The United Nations' interest has at least four aspects: The Holy Places in particular and Palestine in general; the preservation of peace; the validity and efficacy of its own resolutions and other actions; and its specific responsibilities in fields such as refugee administration and the details of peacekeeping.

The role of the United Nations in the Palestine problem raises an important question: can the international community, as represented by a majority in the General Assembly, in fact legislate effectively in the face of determined resistance by any party to the Arab-Israeli dispute? Let us examine this question with particular reference to Jerusalem. Three successive General Assembly resolutions on Jerusalem, all passed with overwhelming majorities, have been virtually ignored. There has been considerable pressure on Israel inside and outside the United Nations forum to moderate its policies. The United States, perhaps Israel's most consistent supporter, termed the annexation a "hasty measure" and stated that it did not consider the laws passed by the Knesset as the final legal solution to the Jerusalem dilemma.[65] Yet despite such extensive disapproval, nothing Israel has said or done since the June war indicates that it has any intention of giving up any part of Jerusalem.

---

[64] See, for example, *Washington Post,* April 30, 1969, p. A 27.
[65] *New York Times,* June 29, 1967.

Much has been written about the nature of community sanctions, the role of the General Assembly as a lawmaking organ, and the ability of the international community to force compliance upon delinquent states. Professor Falk, in discussing General Assembly actions, has suggested the importance of examining "the specifics of the context, especially to determine the relations between the sponsoring majority, the intended and possibly unintended objectives of the resolutions, and the distributions of power in the international society." [66] In other words, who votes for the resolution, and at whom is it directed? Why do states vote for such resolutions? Do they deeply believe that world stability is threatened? Do they want the delinquent state to know of their disapproval? Do they too, under the spotlight of world opinion as their votes are recorded, feel compelled to support a resolution backed by principles of international law and supported by a majority of the world community?

D. H. N. Johnson points out that a resolution may have an important political impact when the U.N. member or members at whom it is directed "run the risk of losing the political friendship and understanding of their fellow Members who voted for the Resolution if they fail to follow the course recommended . . . [or] . . . if it succeeds in affecting the bond between the Government of a state and its own subjects." [67] In 1972 it seemed unlikely that an unfavorable General Assembly resolution would adversely "affect the bond" between the Israeli government and its citizens, a great many of whom tended to be more "hawkish" than the cabinet on issues related to the occupied territories.

Israel declared that the status of Jerusalem was not negotiable—even in the face of United Nations resolutions, international law, and public opinion—and refused to withdraw from occupied territories. The Arab states, on the other hand, adopted the posture of the innocent and injured party, ignoring their role in provoking Israel and hoping that in the dictates of international law and United Nations resolutions they would find the justice they seek. On Jerusalem, even if Israel were to modify its position and accept some sort of international control over the Holy Places, this would fall far short of what has been called for by the United Nations. In the final analysis, the true test of effectiveness of community sanctions is the willingness of states to take action to carry out their resolutions and conventions. Disparity between what states say and what they do can create an international credibility gap of awesome dimensions from the standpoint of international law.

It is sometimes said that the reason for the inability of the world community to reach a solution in the Middle East is that the two superpowers have taken sides. Actually, neither the United States nor the Soviet Union has that much leverage. The somber fact is that none of the region's protagonists has been sufficiently responsive to pressures from the international community. Ultimately, the effectiveness of community sanctions will depend on the willingness and ability of the community itself to procure compliance by a recalcitrant.

---

[66] Richard Falk, "On the Quasi-Legislative Competence of the General Assembly," *American Journal of International Law,* vol. 60 (1966), p. 790.

[67] D. H. N. Johnson, "The Effect of Resolutions of the General Assembly of the U.N.," *British Year Book of International Law,* vol. 32 (1957), p. 121.

The Palestine Refugees

The story of the Palestine refugees does not begin with the outbreak of the Palestine war on May 15, 1948; by that date some 200,000 Palestine Arabs had already become refugees. Nor does it begin with Hitler's persecution and slaughter of the Jewish population of Europe. The seeds were planted, rather, in the late nineteenth century notion that Palestine was "a land without a people for a people without a land" and in the Balfour Declaration of 1917 which gave British support to the establishment of a Jewish "national home."

Palestine was recognized under the British mandate as provisionally independent; Palestinians enjoyed the privileges of citizenship and nationality; they carried Palestinian passports regardless of their faith.[68] Thus, not only were there already people in the land of Palestine: these were people anticipating independent statehood in the near future.

Jewish migration to Palestine grew slowly and steadily under the mandate, and more rapidly after World War II. British officials attempted to control the continued and increasing immigration, which was opposed by the Palestine Arab majority conscious of the conflict between the promises in the Balfour Declaration and Britain's mandatory obligations to the existing population.

In the fighting that began late in 1947 following the General Assembly's partition resolution, the first to leave Palestine for safer territory were almost 30,000 upper- and middle-class Arabs. Their loss seriously crippled many Palestine Arab communities; fear of the growing war and a continuing search for food and shelter prompted thousands of others to follow. Terrorist attacks by the Irgun and the Stern Gang, notably the massacre at the village of Deir Yaseen, stimulated the flow of refugees during the spring of 1948.[69]

The General Assembly adopted a resolution on May 14, 1948, calling for the appointment of a United Nations mediator in Palestine; Count Folke Bernadotte of Sweden was named mediator on May 20. Four months later, on the day before his assassination, Bernadotte submitted a progress report outlining officially for the first time the dimensions of the refugee problem:

> The Arab inhabitants of Palestine are not citizens or subjects of Egypt, Iraq, Lebanon, Syria, and Transjordan, the States which are at present providing them with a refuge and the basic necessities of life. As residents of Palestine, a former mandated territory for which the international community has a continuing responsibility until a final settlement is achieved, these Arab refugees understandably look to the United Nations for effective assistance.

> The right of innocent people, uprooted from their homes by the present terror and ravages of war, to return to their homes, should be affirmed and made effective, with assurance of adequate compensation for the property of those who may choose not to return.[70]

Bernadotte's report stated that "the choice is between saving the lives of many

---

[68] Cherif Bassiouni, "Some Legal Aspects of the Arab-Israeli Conflict," *The Arab World,* vol. 14, no. 10-11 (Special Issue), p. 45.

[69] Khouri, *Arab-Israeli Dilemma,* p. 123.

[70] *UN Year Book, 1947-48,* pp. 305-06, citing General Assembly Document A/648.

thousands of people now or permitting them to die"; he noted also the appeals from Arab states for financial and administrative assistance in coping with the influx of refugees.

A Disaster Relief Project, initiated by Count Bernadotte, was soon replaced by United Nations Relief for Palestine Refugees (UNRPR), established under a General Assembly resolution on November 19, 1948, in which the secretary-general of the UN was requested "to take all necessary steps to extend aid to Palestine refugees and to establish such administrative organization as may be required for this purpose, inviting the assistance of the several Governments, the specialized agencies of the United Nations . . . and other voluntary agencies. . . ." [71] In this resolution it was estimated that $29,500,000 was needed for relief of 500,000 refugees over a nine-month period, plus $2,500,000 for expenses. The secretary-general was authorized to advance up to $5,000,000 from the Working Capital Fund of the United Nations, and member states were urged to make voluntary contributions. (This pattern of short-term finance and major reliance on voluntary contributions has been perpetuated under UNRWA; see below.)

On December 11, 1948, the General Assembly passed another important resolution, laying down the principle of repatriation or compensation (paragraph 11):

> Resolves that the refugees wishing to return to their homes and live at peace with their neighbors should be permitted to do so at the earliest practicable date, and that compensation should be paid for the property of those choosing not to return and for loss of or damage to property which, under the principles of international law or in equity, should be made good by the Governments or authorities responsible.[72]

This same resolution set up a Conciliation Commission to expedite a final peace settlement; it was instructed to "facilitate the repatriation, resettlement and economic and social rehabilitation of the refugees and the payment of compensation." The commission, composed of representatives from France, Turkey and the United States, considered the refugee problem as crucial, for if it could be resolved, solution of other issues might follow.

But the commission found both sides inflexible. According to the Arabs, Israel had not accepted the principle of repatriation, and in any case had made its practical implementation almost impossible in view of the lack of security for Arabs in Israeli-controlled areas and the lack of guarantees of protection of minorities called for under the partition plan. The Arabs complained also that Israel had blocked refugees' bank accounts and had liquidated their real and personal property. The Israeli absentee law was strongly protested. The commission was requested to obtain positive clarification of Israel's position.

Israel, on the other hand, argued that since the resolution specified that refugees who wished to return to their homes should "live at peace with their neighbors," repatriation was contingent on the establishment of peace. Israel did not exclude

---

[71] General Assembly Resolution 212 (III), November 19, 1948.

[72] General Assembly Resolution 194 (III), December 11, 1948; for complete text, see Magnus, *Documents on the Middle East*, p. 161.

the possibility of repatriation of a limited number of refugees, but consistently took the view that solution of the major part of the refugee question lay in resettlement in Arab states.[73]

The General Assembly resolution admitting Israel to the United Nations (May 11, 1949) contains this language:

—Noting that, in the judgment of the Security Council Israel is a peace-loving state and is able and willing to carry out the obligations contained in the Charter . . .

—Noting furthermore the declaration by the State of Israel that it "unreservedly accepts the obligations of the United Nations Charter and undertakes to honour them from the day when it becomes a Member of the United Nations"

—Recalling its Resolutions of 29 December 1947 and 11 December 1948 and taking note of the declarations and explanations made by the representative of the Government of Israel before the ad hoc Political Committee in respect of the implementation of the said resolution . . .

—The General Assembly . . . decides to admit Israel to membership in the United Nations.[74]

The Arab states argued from this that Israel, by ignoring or failing to implement the resolution of December 11, 1948, calling for repatriation, was not living up to its obligations under the Charter.

They also argued that Israel, by its inaction on the refugee problem, violated the Lausanne Protocol of May 12, 1949. This document, signed separately by Israel and several Arab states, accepted as a basis for their discussion with the Conciliation Commission a map showing the territory allocated to the Arab and Jewish states by the partition resolution of 1947. Under the protocol the parties undertook, inter alia, that their exchange of views with the commission would bear upon the territorial adjustments necessary to achieve the various objectives of the resolution of December 11, 1948, including those regarding refugees.[75]

Under pressure from the Conciliation Commission and others, Israel offered to take back 100,000 refugees, but only if it could decide whom to take and where to put them, and only if the Arabs at the same time agreed to a final peace settlement. The commission found this offer unacceptable, as did the Arab states. Jordan and Syria announced that they could accept refugees who did not want to go home; Egypt and Lebanon, however, protested that they were already over-crowded and could not do so. Some agreement was reached on the issue of blocked bank accounts, and Israel agreed to a "reunion of families" plan (although disagreements arose over the definition of "family").

These steps, however, represented so little progress that a new approach was tried. On August 29, 1949, a United Nations Economic Survey Mission for the Middle East (the Clapp mission) was established to undertake a study of prob-

[73] *UN Year Book, 1948-49*, pp. 203-04.
[74] General Assembly Resolution 273 (III), May 11, 1949.
[75] United Nations, *Annual Report of the Secretary-General on the Work of the Organization, 1 July 1948 - 30 June 1949* (1949), p. 5.

lems relating to repatriation, resettlement, and social and economic rehabilitation of the refugees. In an interim report (November 16, 1949) the mission stated that the refugees themselves were the most serious manifestation of economic dislocation created by the Palestine hostilities. Acknowledging that repatriation required political decisions outside its competence, the mission suggested that the most constructive course immediately available was to give the refugees an opportunity to find work under existing conditions. It recommended setting up a special agency for this purpose.[76] Accordingly, less than a month later, the General Assembly established the United Nations Relief and Works Agency for Palestine Refugees in the Near East (UNRWA) to take over the functions of UNRPR. In the enabling resolution, it was recognized that

> . . . without prejudice to the provisions of paragraph 11 of the General Assembly Resolution 194 (III) of 11 December 1948, continued assistance for the relief of the Palestine refugees is necessary to prevent conditions of starvation and distress among them and to further conditions of peace and stability, and that constructive measures should be undertaken at an early date with a view to the termination of international assistance for relief.[77]

UNRWA was authorized to spend up to $54,900,000 on a relief program lasting a year and a half. By the following May it had launched a comprehensive program of welfare and public services, including food, clothing, shelter, medical care, education, vocational training, and special hardship assistance. UNRWA has been in operation ever since.

The exact number of refugees created by the 1948-49 hostilities has been a matter of dispute. The Clapp mission estimated that 726,000 persons had been dislocated as a direct result of the war. In June 1965, 1,280,823 were registered with UNRWA, of whom 54 percent lived in Jordan, mainly on the West Bank. The Jordanian Government granted them full citizenship. Another 25 percent lived in the Gaza Strip, under Egyptian administration but remote from Egypt's main population centers. Lebanon, with 11 percent, was not in a strong position politically or economically to assist them. Syria, which has less of a population problem, was host for about 135,000 refugees (as of 1965), mostly homeless and economically unproductive. It should be noted that these UNRWA rolls do not cover everyone made homeless by the 1948 war, since they include only those who had lived in Palestine for at least two years prior thereto, and who lost both their home and their means of livelihood. "Economic refugees," those who lost their jobs but not their homes, are excluded.

When UNRWA was established in 1949 it was instructed by the General Assembly to "continue to endeavor to reduce the number of rations by progressive stages." Rectification of the relief rolls has been a problem ever since. In September 1964 UNRWA Commissioner-General Michelmore pledged to intensify the agency's efforts; he pointed out that if host governments and refugees cooperated in removing ineligible persons from the rolls, funds could be released to provide rations for children on the waiting lists. The host governments agreed in principle,

---

[76] *UN Year Book, 1948-49,* p. 209.
[77] General Assembly Resolution 302 (IV), December 8, 1949.

in return for a broadened definition of needy refugees; but the governments contributing most of UNRWA's funds balked at the latter. Problems such as this remain unresolved.

UNRWA's expenses are not part of the regular United Nations budget. The agency has depended on voluntary contributions, which from 1950 to 1970 totaled more than $708 million. Four countries contributed almost 90 percent of that total: the United States $477.9 million (67 percent), United Kingdom $114 million, Canada $25.9 million, and France $16.1 million. There has also been assistance from other sources; for instance, the International Committee of the Red Cross, the League of Red Cross Societies, and the American Friends Service Committee have all assumed considerable responsibility for the distribution of supplies.

Who is Responsible for the Refugees? According to Israel, the Arab leaders caused the refugee problem by prolonging the fighting in 1948-49 and by urging Palestinians in numerous radio broadcasts to leave their homes and country to join the United Arab Army which would take Palestine back from the Zionists. The Arab states, on the other hand, insist that the Palestinians were, in fact, urged to remain in their villages. The whole truth may never be known. According to Professor Khouri,

> Erskine B. Childers, a British journalist, made an intensive effort to find some proof of the existence of the alleged orders. He interviewed Arab leaders, checked the monitored broadcasts made during the months involved, and asked Israeli officials to show him whatever documentary proof they had concerning these claims. After his investigation, Childers reported that he found "not a single order, or appeal, or support about evacuation from Palestine from any Arab nation, inside or outside of Palestine, in 1948." In fact, there was "repeated monitory record of Arab appeals, even flat orders, to the civilians of Palestine to stay put" and not to leave.[78]

From the refugee standpoint the conflicting assertions are really beside the point. As Dr. John Badeau has realistically pointed out, when one is surrounded by fighting and is threatened with death or hunger, one needs little encouragement, from friends or enemies, to escape the situation. At all events, hundreds of thousands of refugees were living outside Israel's boundaries within a year after it had been proclaimed a state. Their ranks continued to swell; in the fall of 1950 and later in the summer of 1953 many Palestinians, the majority of them Bedouin, were forced to leave, and in 1951 many Arabs living in the Israeli-Syrian demilitarized zone abandoned their homes.[79]

The Arab states argue that since Israel and the United Nations are responsible for the refugee problem, it is they who must solve it. However, as indicated by Khouri, Palestinian leaders share the blame: not only did they not prepare their people for the war or its aftermath; many of them fled Palestine before May 1948,

---

[78] Khouri, *Arab-Israeli Dilemma*, p. 389n., citing Erskine B. Childers, "The Other Exodus," *The Spectator* (London), May 21, 1961.

[79] Khouri, *Arab-Israeli Dilemma*, p. 125, citing Security Council Documents C/1797, S/2234, and S/2300.

leaving the people without leadership. UNRWA's attitude is that "blame" is a secondary matter. Whether the Palestinians were urged or compelled to leave, whether they fled to avoid the fighting or to find food, does not alter the statistics: for whatever reasons, about 700,000 Palestinians became refugees in 1948 and 1949.

How Can the Problem be Resolved? Israel argues that there can be no settlement of the refugee problem—whether by repatriation, resettlement or compensation—except as part of a final peace settlement with international guarantees for Israel's security. The Arab states, on the other hand, regard the refugee question as central; peace is not possible until the Palestinian problem is resolved. Pragmatic steps such as the Clapp mission, UNRPR and UNRWA have been helpful but insufficient; the Arab states rely on the moral and legal weight of successive General Assembly resolutions in calling for a total approach to the problem—political, social and legal, as well as economic. Demands by Israel and others that UNRWA phase out its operations have made the Arab states wary that if they once cooperate in large-scale development projects, UNRWA will find cause to reduce its own share in such operations. Moreover, there is a fear that the establishment of permanent schools, hospitals and training centers for the refugees will be interpreted as acceptance of the idea of resettlement, and the pressure for repatriation will be taken off Israel.

The Arab states argue, and United Nations surveys confirm, that they are already overpopulated and severely lacking in the resources needed to assimilate a million homeless people with little in the way of productive resources of their own. Professor Khouri observes: "Only a large-scale economic development program for the whole Middle East could have made possible the integration of all the refugees into the economic life of the area, without, at the same time, seriously impairing the economic interests of the indigenous populations." [80] Israel contends, however, that some Arab states, at least, have the space and resources to absorb the Palestinians, who would be happier settled among their Arab brethren. Khouri regards this as an over-simplification:

> . . . in the fields of economic and political development, the refugees had more in common with most Israelis than with Arabs who lived in such places as Yemen and Oman. . . . If the refugees had been given a completely free choice, they would naturally have wished to live within an Arab state of Palestine. If denied this choice, they would then have preferred to settle among those Arabs with whom they had most in common. These Arabs resided in Lebanon (already over-crowded and afflicted with a delicate political balance between Christians and Muslims), Jordan (also seriously over-crowded), Syria and Israel.[81]

Repatriation. Paragraph 11 of Resolution 194 (III) of 1948 calls for the repatriation of "refugees wishing to return to their homes and live at peace with their neighbors." Who is to determine whether a particular refugee wishes to "live at peace"? Israel has contended that the security risk of admitting hostile refugees is

---

[80] Khouri, *Arab-Israeli Dilemma*, p. 164.
[81] Ibid.

59

too great. Khouri suggests, based on United Nations and United States reports, that the most likely candidates would be people seeking to rejoin their families, who would be unlikely to "rock the boat." It has also been suggested that refugees choosing to return could begin to bridge the gap between the Arab states and Israel, and their return would symbolize progress toward Middle Eastern reconciliation. In any case, the presence of so many irredentist-minded Palestinians on Israel's borders may constitute a greater security risk than their peaceful, or at least pacified, resettlement within Israel's borders. An American diplomat once commented:

> I do not think that it is in the interest of the Arab states that a generation is growing up convinced that they must seek by war a solution to problems which were created by war. I do not think that it is in the interest of Israel that a generation is growing up in isolation from the peoples and cultures of the areas where Israel must live and convinced that for the indefinite future they must stand on the ramparts of a garrison state.[82]

Compensation. Included in all the resolutions dealing with the refugee problem have been provisions for compensation for property lost, destroyed or confiscated. The issue of compensation—how much and for whom—has occupied a great deal of the time and attention of mediation teams in the Middle East, perhaps because it is one step removed from the more sensitive problems involved in the actual movement of people. The Arab position is that such compensation must be adequate, and that Israel has an unqualified obligation to pay. Israel argues that compensation is required only as part of a final peace settlement, that it would require substantial international financial assistance, and that payment of a lump sum must operate as a release from all claims by individual refugees. Furthermore, Israel contends that property of Israeli citizens in Iraq, in the old Jewish quarter of Jerusalem, and in other Arab countries must be taken into account, as well as the economic effects of the continuing Arab boycott on Israel's economy.

The Role of the Palestinians. The annual reaffirmations by the General Assembly of the Palestinians' rights of repatriation serve to keep their hopes alive. But the refugees have unfortunately become a sort of political football. The Arab states, says Israel, publicize the plight of the refugees to turn world opinion against the Israelis; they have been less than frank with the refugees about conditions under which they might be repatriated. But Israel has also used the refugees as a debating point with the Arabs: settlement of the refugee problem is inevitably made contingent on a final peace settlement. (At one point Israel offered to take all the refugees in Gaza, if the Gaza Strip itself were also included in the "deal." [83] The Palestinians themselves have also put pressure on the various Arab host governments to take extreme and hostile positions—for instance, to bypass the provision stipulating *peaceful* repatriation.

All of this is not to imply that refugee repatriation is the sort of issue that has to

---

[82] Donald C. Bergus, "Palestine: Focal Point of Tension," *Department of State Bulletin,* March 26, 1956, p. 505.

[83] Khouri, *Arab-Israeli Dilemma,* p. 128.

be worked at to be kept alive. On the contrary: many Palestinian refugee camps lie near the Israeli border. In some cases the refugees can actually see their homes, or at least the spot where their homes once stood. Given the reluctance or inability of Arab governments to encourage full integration into their own states, the unrepatriated refugee is a vital figure in the tense situation along Israel's frontiers.

Repatriation, compensation and settlement have come to be discussed not so much in terms of their legal validity or practicability as in terms of the numbers of people involved in any such solutions. The lexicon has proliferated to the point where one must distinguish between "old" and "new" refugees, and even between old and new "displaced non-refugees." An example is Secretary-General U Thant's report to the General Assembly and the Security Council following the June war:

> The Secretary-General stated that some 113,000 refugees previously registered with UNRWA had been displaced, of whom the largest number—about 93,000—had moved from the west bank of the Jordan River to the east bank. Another 17,000 had moved from the south-western corner of Syria to Damascus and Der'a, and some 3,000 former residents of the Gaza Strip were in the United Arab Republic. Even larger numbers—210,000—of persons not previously registered with UNRWA were also displaced. About 85,000 of these displaced persons moved from the western to the eastern side of the Jordan, about 90,000 from the southern part of Syria to Damascus and Der'a, and a further 35,000 from Sinai westward across the Suez Canal. . . . The Secretary-General . . . stated that the immediate needs of food, shelter, and health service of some 325,000 people displaced from areas now occupied by Israel as a result of the conflict in June were being met.[84]

In a useful analysis of the current problem, Professor Khouri has identified three main population shifts following the June war. Two comprise groups that are in Israel or Israeli-held territory today: Arabs from Jerusalem who moved to the West Bank to avoid the fighting or Israeli administration; and some 550,000 "old" refugees who remained on the West Bank. The third group—300,000 new refugees in the United Arab Republic, Jordan, and Syria—are the subject of entirely new demands for repatriation. In August 1967 the Red Cross promoted an agreement between Israel and Jordan for repatriation of refugees to the West Bank. At that time about 32,000 families, totaling about 160,000 persons, applied to return to the West Bank, and facilities for receiving applications were kept open.[85] However, as of December 1968, only about 20,000 had been allowed to return, while at the same time many Arab leaders and professionals were moving in the other direction, out of Israeli-held territory.[86]

Since 1967 Israel has been observed to be less critical of UNRWA than formerly, and less anxious to see it terminate its operations—a shift in position which is perhaps understandable now that about forty percent of all Palestinian refugees are living within Israel's new frontiers. Israel continues to oppose repatri-

---

[84] *UN Monthly Chronicle,* September 1967, p. 31.
[85] Ibid.
[86] *UN Monthly Chronicle,* January 1969, p. 85.

ation of "old" refugees and argues that there is no longer room for them; in December 1968 it offered to allow 7,000 persons to return, but the offer was derided by the Arabs as a mere token. At the same time, Israel continues to call for more Jewish immigration. Newly occupied areas, for the most part, are being inhabited by new Jewish immigrants.[87]

United Nations resolutions continue to play an important part in the refugee debate. Security Council Resolution 242 of November 22, 1967, which has been generally accepted by the international community as containing all the essential ingredients for an ultimate resolution of the Arab-Israeli conflict, calls simply but clearly for a "just settlement of the refugee problem." A General Assembly resolution of December 13, 1968, noted

> with deep regret that repatriation or compensation of the refugees as provided for in paragraph 11 of General Assembly Resolution 194 (III) has not been effected, that no substantial progress has been made in the programme endorsed in paragraph 2 of Resolution 513 (VI) for the reintegration of refugees by repatriation or resettlement and that, therefore, the situation of the refugees continues to be a matter of serious concern.[88]

The resolution called upon Israel to take effective steps for the return of persons who fled their homes and camps as a result of the June war. At the safe time the assembly passed further resolutions extending UNRWA's mandate until June 30, 1972, endorsing the efforts of the commissioner-general, and appealing urgently for generous contributions from member governments to meet the continuing needs of the agency.[89]

The Palestinians themselves have emerged as a major party to the refugee debate. No longer content to be represented by their Arab hosts, they have asserted a new Palestinian nationalism. Many are now convinced that they relied too long upon other Arab states without success, and now they alone can help themselves. Positions taken by the Palestinians bear a certain resemblance to the positions adopted by Arab delegations at the United Nations following the Palestine War in 1948. Following is an official summary of part of a discussion that took place in the Special Political Committee of the United Nations late in 1968:

> A Representative of the Palestine Arab delegation—to whom the Committee granted a hearing on the understanding that such authorization did not constitute recognition of the organization represented—said the Palestine Arab refugees rejected *in toto* the Security Council Resolution of 22 November 1967 on the Middle East. The refugees, he said, were determined to resist any settlement which deprived them of their inalienable right to self-determination and of their right to return to their ancestral homeland. Similarly, the refugees were also determined to resist any Arab state or any Arab leader who might be forced to submit to the pressure of the Great Powers . . . .
>
> The Palestine Arab delegation proposed a 10-point programme for a just and peaceful settlement of the Middle East problem. The pro-

[87] Ibid., p. 81.
[88] General Assembly Resolution A/RES/2341 (XXII), December 13, 1968.
[89] *UN Monthly Chronicle,* January 1969, p. 79.

gramme included: the Security Council, in accordance with the Charter and the principles of international law, must decide that the proclamation of a "Jewish State" in Palestine is null and void *ab initio;* the Council must also expel Israel from the United Nations, take measures to disarm the illegal Jewish colonial regime in Palestine, declare an embargo on arms and munitions to that regime, call on all Member State to sever diplomatic relations with that regime . . . .

The General Assembly should set up a United Nations Commission to facilitate the repatriation of the Palestine Jewish immigrants to their homes . . . and another commission to facilitate the return of the Palestinians to their home.

The Palestine Arabs were not against Jews. He added that the intention of the Palestine Arabs was to liberate Jews from Zionist domination and to welcome all Jews who would like to live in an Arab state as citizens enjoying equal rights under law and the Constitution.[90]

While the practical possibility of implementing a program as extreme as this must be regarded as highly unrealistic, to say the least, it would be unwise to disregard the feelings and emotions that lie behind it. The Palestinian nationalist movement has a strong hold on the imagination and commitment of young people throughout the Arab world. Unlike other revolutionary movements that appear to exist for the revolution's own sake, Palestinian nationalism is part of the larger network of Arab nationalism. The emergence of the Palestinians as a self-conscious national group after 1967 was probably inevitable. At all events, an end to the woes of the individual Arab refugee still appears as remote as ever.

---

[90] Ibid., pp. 83-84.

IV. PASSAGE THROUGH INTERNATIONAL WATERWAYS

Many international waterways, natural or artificial, serve the Middle East. Some, like the Turkish Straits, the Suez Canal, the Bab el Mandeb and the Straits of Hodmuz, are vital passages for the commerce of the world; they cut across continents or connect one major international body of water with another. Others, such as the Straits of Tiran and the Shatt al-Arab, are less important only in the sense that the interests of fewer states are involved; such interests, nevertheless, have often conflicted. Some of the problems connected with the waterways—for instance, the one involving the Straits of Tiran—have developed only recently; but others, such as the Turkish Straits and the Suez Canal, have their origins in the last century or even earlier times. Still others (Bab el Mandeb, Straits of Hormuz) represent only potential problems that hopefully may never arise. In this discussion of the navigable waterways of the region the emphasis will be placed on those that have in one way or another become the subject of international interest or concern from the legal and diplomatic standpoint.

The Turkish Straits

The control of the Turkish Straits has constituted one of the major themes of diplomatic history and international law. The straits problem is as old as ancient Greece. In modern times it has involved reconciliation of Turkey's sovereignty over the territory surrounding the straits with the interests of other nations desiring either to make use of them or to deny their use to others. Their present status, which does not appear to be a matter of significant dispute in the legal sense, was achieved largely through channels of conventional diplomacy guided by recognized international legal standards. This example may be instructive when one comes to consider the present issues surrounding another equally important waterway in a somewhat similar geographical situation: the Suez Canal. (See the following section.)

The Turkish Straits include the Sea of Marmara, which lies between the Dardanelles to the southwest, the waterway leading to the Aegean Sea, and the Bosporus to the northeast, the waterway leading to the Black Sea. The Bosporus is about 18 miles long, and its width varies from a minimum of about 800 yards to about two and three-quarters miles at the Black Sea entrance. The Dardanelles are about 47 miles long, and their width averages three to four miles. These waterways are important economically and strategically: economically because they provide water routes for commerce between the countries of the Black Sea and the rest of the world; and strategically because they serve as a checkpoint against any power (or powers) which controls the Black Sea and seeks an outlet to the Mediterranean. Conversely, the straits provide a potential barrier to any power (or powers) which may seek access to the Black Sea.

Following Turkish occupation of the Balkans and the Black Sea in the fifteenth century, the Ottoman Porte prohibited the passage of foreign ships into the straits and the Black Sea without permission. The principle of interdiction, based on Ottoman control of the straits and the Black Sea (which is landlocked) became a principle of Turkish public law, and Turkish control remained uncontested until Russia began to gain a foothold on the northern Black Sea coasts.[1] The first international instrument granting Russia the right of passage was the Treaty of Küchük Kainarja, concluded in 1774 between Russia and Turkey. In this treaty Russia was not only recognized as a Black Sea power and granted an access to the Mediterranean, but also obtained trade privileges on an equal footing with other most-favored nations.[2] The Black Sea was no longer an inland sea. Russia's rights of passage through the straits were embodied in Article XI:

> There shall be a free and unimpeded navigation for the merchant ships belonging to the two Contracting Powers, in all the seas which wash their shores; the Sublime Porte grants to Russian merchant-vessels . . . a free passage from the Black Sea into the White Sea [Aegean] . . . as also the power of entering all ports and harbours situated either on the sea-coasts, or in the passages and channels which join those seas.[3]

A *convention explicative* relating to this treaty, concluded in 1779, confirmed Russian rights of passage. The ancient rule of Ottoman closure of the Turkish Straits was modified, but Ottoman jurisdiction over the straits remained unimpaired. Subsequent treaties between Russia and the Ottoman Porte confirmed the principle of the opening of the straits to merchant vessels of other nations with whom there were agreements granting such rights.[4] By the middle of the 19th century rights of passage were claimed by all the capitulatory powers. In the Treaty of Paris of 1856, the principle of free commercial navigation became universal. Article XI recognized that the waters and ports of the Black Sea were "thrown open to the mercantile marine of every nation"; and Article XII provided: "Free from any impediment, the commerce in the ports and waters of the Black Sea shall be subject only to regulations of health, customs, and police, framed in a spirit favorable to the development of commercial transactions."[5]

---

[1] For a discussion of early Ottoman practice, see Erik Bruel, *International Straits: A Treatise on International Law,* vol. II (Copenhagen, 1947), pp. 252-72.

[2] In 1535 France obtained privileges referred to as capitulations; these privileges, later extended to various other European powers, placed certain restraints on Turkish sovereignty, especially in connection with the protection of minorities. For the origins and nature of the capitulations, see Majid Khadduri and Herbert Liebesny, eds., *Law in the Middle East* (Washington, 1955), Chapter 13.

[3] Text of Treaty of Küchük Kainarja in J. C. Hurewitz, *Diplomacy in the Near and Middle East* (Princeton, 1956), vol. I, pp. 54-61.

[4] Bruel, *International Straits,* pp. 272-76; Y. M. Altug, *Turkey and Some Problems of International Law* (Istanbul, 1958), pp. 41ff. For problems encountered by American merchant and naval vessels before the establishment of diplomatic relations with Turkey in 1831, see David H. Finnie, *Pioneers East: The Early American Experience in the Middle East* (Cambridge: Harvard University Press, 1967), Chapter 3.

[5] Hurewitz, *Diplomacy,* vol. I, p. 155.

TURKISH STRAITS

BULGARIA

Ivaylovgrad

Komotini

GREECE

Alexandroupolis

Orestias

Edirne

Kirklareli

Vize

Babaeski

Luleburgaz

Uzunkopru

Midye

Karacakoy

Corlu

TURKEY

Kesan

Inecik

Tekirdag

Silivri

Sariyer

Karakoy

Enez

Sarkoy

(Gelibolu) Gallipoli

Martisa R.

Dardanelles

Eceabat

Lemnos I.

Aegean Sea

Imroz I.

Samothrace I.

Kumkale

Dardanelles

Canakkale

Lapseki

Ayvacik

Edremit

Biga

Can

Gonen

Bugdayho

L. Kus

Karacabey

Simau R.

Balya

Balikesir

Avsa I.

Erdek I.

Erdek

Bandirma

Marmara I.

Imrali I.

Sea of Marmara

Princess Is.

Istanbul

Uskudar

Beykoz

Kadikoy

Bosporus

Sile

Izmit

Golcuk

Yalova

Gemlik

L. Iznik

Yenisehir

Inegol

Bursa

TURKEY

OrhaneliO

Orhaneli R.

L. Ulubat

Black Sea

The question of commercial navigation through the straits having been laid to rest, there remained the perennial problem of the transit of war vessels. In 1833 the Russian fleet was allowed passage, a right denied to other nations. This, at least, was the Russian interpretation of the Treaty of Hunkiar Iskelesi, tacitly accepted by Turkish commentators.[6] But recent research has shown that the passage rights to Russian warships were not unqualified and were not necessarily accepted by other powers.[7] In 1841 the following formula was adopted in the Straits Convention of London:

(1) War vessels of foreign powers were prohibited from entering the straits in accordance with the "ancient rule" of the Ottoman Empire, so long as the Ottoman Porte was at peace;

(2) However, the sultan reserved the right "to deliver *firmans* [i.e., decrees granting licenses] of passage for light vessels under the flag of war, which shall be employed as is usual in the service of the Missions of Foreign Powers." [8]

This formula remained operative, generally speaking, until World War I, although Russia continued to try to obtain special privileges. The Black Sea was neutralized by the Treaty of Paris of 1856, limiting Russia's opportunities to send warships through the straits.[9] This neutralization was removed in the Treaty of London (1871); however, the straits remained closed in principle to war vessels, though the sultan was granted wider latitude to issue *firmans*.[10] After unsuccessful Russian attempts to gain further privileges (San Stefano, 1877), the provisions of the Treaties of Paris (1856) and London (1871) were confirmed by the Treaty of Berlin of 1878.[11] This rule remained operative until 1914.[12]

During World War I, the straits were closed to the Allied Powers, since Turkey had joined the Central Powers and had extended privileges only to Germany and its allies.[13] Russia, now an ally of Britain and France, sought once again the advantages she had tried for so often. In the secret Constantinople "agreement" of 1915 among the Entente powers, Russia was virtually promised control of the straits as well as other territorial advantages in the event of victory; but these undertakings, such as they were, lapsed with the advent of the Soviet regime and Russia's withdrawal from the war. [14]

Following World War I, the victorious allies tried in the Treaty of Sèvres to

---

[6] Sergei Goriainov, *Le Bosphore et les Dardanelles* (Paris, 1910); Altug, *Some Problems of International Law*, p. 48.

[7] P. E. Mosely, *Russian Diplomacy and the Opening of the Eastern Question in 1838 and 1839* (Cambridge, 1934); J. C. Hurewitz, "The Background of Russia's Claims to the Turkish Straits," *Bulletin, Turk Tarih Kurumu Basimevi*, vol. 28 (1963), pp. 462-503.

[8] Text in Hurewitz, *Diplomacy*, vol. I, p. 123.

[9] Since the Black Sea was neutralized, Russian war vessels were allowed passage neither through the Black Sea nor through the straits (See Articles XI-XIV.)

[10] Text in Hurewitz, *Diplomacy*, vol. I, pp. 173-74.

[11] Ibid., pp. 189-91.

[12] For an account of the theory and practice of this rule, see Bruel, *International Straits*, pp. 289-315.

[13] Ibid., pp. 315ff.

[14] For texts and discussion of these negotiations, see H. W. V. Temperley, *A History of the Peace Conference of Paris* (London, 1924), vol. VI, Chapter 1.

establish a new regime for the straits in which the navigation "shall in the future be open, both in peace and war, to every vessel of commerce or of war, and to military and commercial aircraft, without distinction of flag." This regime was to be placed under the control of a "Commission of the Straits," composed of representatives of up to ten nations including the United States.[15] However, the Treaty of Sèvres was never ratified by Turkey and was repudiated by the new Kemalist government.

With the Treaty of Lausanne (1923), which Turkey did ratify (though Russia did not), Turkey's agreement was obtained to the principle of free transit and navigation by sea and air without compromising her sovereignty or control over the straits zone.[16] However, this zone was to be demilitarized. Navigation for both commercial and war vessels and aircraft, in time of peace and time of war, was spelled out in elaborate rules. All merchant vessels and nonmilitary aircraft were granted complete freedom of navigation in time of peace, and also in time of war if Turkey remained neutral. If Turkey were a belligerent, however, freedom of navigation would be enjoyed by neutral merchant vessels and neutral nonmilitary aircraft only if they did not assist the enemy, particularly by carrying contraband, troops or enemy nationals, and Turkey had the right of visit and search. Moreover, as a belligerent, Turkey had the right to deny access to the straits to enemy merchant vessels.

Under this convention warships and military aircraft were granted complete freedom of navigation in time of peace, subject to the following restrictions as to the "total force":

> The maximum force which any one Power may send through the Straits into the Black Sea is not to be greater than that of the most powerful fleet of the littoral Powers of the Black Sea existing in that sea at the time of passage; but with the proviso that the Powers reserve to themselves the right to send into the Black Sea, at any time and under all circumstances, a force of not more than three ships, of which no individual ship shall exceed 10,000 tons.

In time of war and if Turkey was neutral, the same rules applied except that the restrictions as to total force "will not be applicable to any belligerent Power to the prejudice of its belligerent rights in the Black Sea." As a neutral, Turkey could not take any measure that interfered with navigation through the straits, but the warships and military aircraft of belligerents were forbidden to carry out hostile acts such as search and visit. In case Turkey were a belligerent, complete freedom of passage (subject to the total force restrictions) would be granted to neutral warships and no measure could be taken to interfere with their free passage.

Passage of the straits by submarines had to be made on the surface. The commander of a naval force approaching the straits from either direction was required to signal to a shore station as he entered, giving the number and the names of the vessels under his command. Warships could not remain during their

---

[15] Text in Hurewitz, *Diplomacy*, vol. II, pp. 81-82.

[16] These arrangements were embodied in a "Convention on the Regime of the Straits," which was one of the Lausanne instruments. See Bruel, *International Straits*, pp. 359-88; Hurewitz, *Diplomacy*, vol. II, pp. 124-27.

transit beyond the time necessary to effect their passage except in case of damage or peril of the sea. Finally, the 1923 convention set up an international "Straits Commission," with the Turkish representative as President, to supervise the execution of the convention and report regularly to the League of Nations.

This regime was modified substantially, at Turkey's initiative, by the Montreux Convention of 1936. Turkey took over the functions of the Straits Commission (see above), was authorized to remilitarize the area, and was given greater discretion to regulate passage of foreign war vessels. The Montreux Convention also granted the Black Sea powers greater privileges than those enjoyed by other nations, in terms of the number and tonnage of vessels permitted to pass through the straits. In time of war and if Turkey was a belligerent, or (significantly) if Turkey "considered herself to be threatened with imminent danger of war," the passage of warships was left entirely to the discretion of the Turkish government.[17]

The reasons prompting Turkey to demand these modifications were political and strategic; it should be noted that Turkey's position had the support of Britain, France and the Soviet Union at a time when the Axis Powers began to present a threat to the status quo in the Mediterranean.[18]

The Straits: Cold War Developments. The Montreux Convention, which came into force on November 9, 1936, provided that any party could initiate proposals for amendments at the end of any five-year period, and set up machinery for dealing with such proposals (Article 29). At the Big Three conference at Yalta in February 1945 the United States and Britain accepted a Soviet suggestion that proposals for revision of the 1936 convention would be tabled at their next meeting. At the next conference at Potsdam (July-August 1945) it was agreed that the 1936 convention "should be revised, as failing to meet present-day conditions." [19] It was also agreed that the matter would be the subject of direct communications between each of the three Big Powers and the Turkish government. Following Potsdam there was a lively interchange of notes on the future regime of the Turkish Straits. The Soviet Union, essentially, was trying to establish a new regime under the joint control of Turkey and the Soviet Union. The United States, in a note of November 2, 1945, put forward the following proposals:

(1) The straits to be open to the merchant vessels of all nations at all times.

(2) The straits to be open to the transit of warships of Black Sea powers at all times.

(3) Save for an agreed limited tonnage in time of peace, passage through the straits to be denied to the warships of non-Black Sea powers at all times, except with the specific consent of the Black Sea powers or except when acting under the authority of the United Nations.

[17] Bruel, *International Straits*, pp. 388-406; Hurewitz, *Diplomacy*, vol. II, pp. 197-203.

[18] See Cemil Bilsel, "International Law in Turkey," *American Journal of International Law*, vol. 38 (1944), pp. 546-56. For developments leading to the Montreux Convention, see A. J. Toynbee, *Survey of International Affairs, 1936* (London, 1937), pp. 584-641.

[19] For British and American attitudes, see Stephen G. Xydis, "New Light on the Big Three Crisis over Turkey in 1945," *Middle East Journal*, vol. 14 (1960), pp. 416-32.

(4) Certain changes to modernize the Montreux Convention, such as the substitution of the United Nations system for that of the League of Nations and the elimination of Japan as a signatory.[20]

The British government endorsed the American proposals in a note dated November 21, 1945, and the Turkish reply, in welcoming these proposals, stated that Turkey would accept the decisions of an international conference provided that "Turkey's independence, sovereignty and territorial integrity are not infringed."

But these proposals, favorable as they were to the Black Sea powers, did not go far enough to satisfy the Soviet Union. On August 7, 1946, the Soviet government presented to Turkey a note containing its own proposals. The note began by reciting a number of incidents which made it "obvious" that the Montreux Convention had not prevented Germany and its allies from using the straits for military purposes during World War II. The Soviet note proposed a "new regime" based on the following principles:

(1) The straits should be always open to the passage of merchant ships of all countries.

(2) The straits should be always open to the passage of warships of Black Sea powers.

(3) Passage through the straits for warships not belonging to the Black Sea powers should not be permitted except in cases specially provided for.

(4) The establishment of a regime of the straits, as the sole sea passage leading from the Black Sea and to the Black Sea, should come under the competence of Turkey and other Black Sea powers.

(5) Turkey and the Soviet Union, as the powers most interested and capable of guaranteeing freedom to commercial navigation and security in the straits, should organize joint means of defense of the straits for the prevention of the utilization of the straits by other countries for aims hostile to the Black Sea powers.[21]

The Soviet note was unacceptable to the United States, Britain and Turkey. The Turkish reply, dated August 22, 1946, referred first to the allegations regarding the passage of Axis vessels, which it dismissed as inapplicable or trivial. With regard to the Soviet Union's five points, Turkey expressed its readiness to revise the Montreux Convention to adapt it to meet technical development and changed conditions, but it rejected points 4 and 5 as being incompatible with Turkish sovereignty and security. The United States and Britain supported Turkey fully in this position, and except for a further round of diplomatic notes [22] nothing more was done. The Montreux Convention remains in force. The political and military support furnished by the United States to Turkey, beginning with the Truman

---

[20] For texts of the diplomatic correspondence, see annexes of Department of State, *The Problem of the Turkish Straits* (Washington, 1947), prepared by Harry N. Howard, pp. 47ff.
[21] Ibid., pp. 47-49.
[22] Ibid., pp. 50-58.

Doctrine in 1947, has undoubtedly figured significantly in this result.[23] Turkey's rights to control the straits have been protected.

The Suez Canal

Egypt's closure of the Suez Canal to Israeli shipping has been an issue since the establishment of Israel in 1948. Although the closure was not an immediate cause of the June war of 1967, Israel insisted upon resolution of the canal-closure problem as part of a settlement. In its historic Resolution 242 of November 22, 1967, the United Nations Security Council, without referring specifically to the canal, affirmed among other things "the necessity for guaranteeing freedom of navigation through international waterways in the area." The matter is therefore a live one, despite the physical closure of the canal since the June war. Consideration is given here chiefly to legal positions that have been adopted by Israel and Egypt, respectively. The issues are by no means as straightforward as might be supposed at first glance.

The Israeli Position. Israel has consistently demanded the right of free passage through the Suez Canal enjoyed by other nations, claiming that Egypt's closure of the canal to its shipping runs contrary to general principles of international law, the Constantinople Convention of 1888,[24] and Israel's armistice agreement with Egypt of 1949. Under general principles of international law, Israel claims the right to navigate freely on the high seas, through international waterways that connect high seas, and through international rivers. Such rights, in Israel's view, constitute a "cornerstone" of international law which cannot be denied to it as one of the members of the community of nations.

The Constantinople Convention of 1888, which is the basic instrument governing international rights and obligations relating to the Suez Canal, provides (Article I) that the canal "shall always be free and open, in time of war as in time of peace, to every vessel of commerce or of war, without distinction of flag." Israel regards Egypt's restrictive measures as contrary to the terms of this convention and therefore illegal. Israel has claimed, at least inferentially, that the convention prohibits Egypt from taking defensive measures in the canal area to the extent that they interfere with the right of free passage;[25] Egypt's justification based on the existence of a state of war with Israel is countered not only on the basis of Article I but also on the ground that no other state—except the Arab states— recognizes that such a state of war exists. On the contrary, the United Nations on more than one occasion has called upon Egypt to open the canal to Israeli shipping. The rationale is that Egypt and Israel, having accepted the obligations of the United Nations Charter, cannot remain at war with each other. If they ever

---

[23] For American-Turkish relations since World War II, see Harry S. Truman, *Memoirs,* vol. II (New York, 1956), pp. 96-109; George F. Kennan, *Memoirs, 1925-1950* (Boston, 1967), pp. 313-24; George Kirk, *Survey of International Affairs: The Middle East, 1945-1950* (London, 1954), pp. 21-56.

[24] Text in Hurewitz, *Diplomacy,* vol. I, pp. 202-05; see also Ralph H. Magnus, ed., *Documents on the Middle East* (Washington, D.C.: American Enterprise Institute for Public Policy Research, 1969), pp. 8-11.

[25] UN Security Council, 658th meeting (1954), p. 9. See also Benno Avram, *The Evolution of the Suez Canal Status from 1869 Up To 1956* (Geneva, 1958), pp. 119-21.

SUEZ CANAL

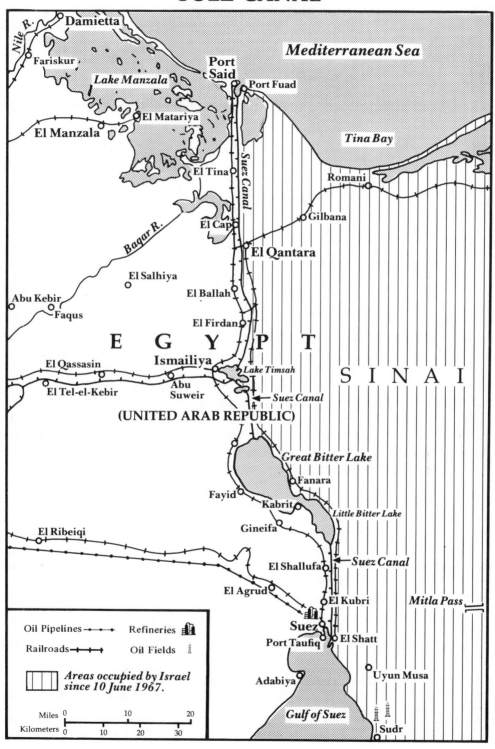

Damietta
Nile R.
Fariskur
Lake Manzala
Port Said
Port Fuad
Mediterranean Sea

El Matariya
El Manzala
Tina Bay

El Tina
Suez Canal
Romani

Baqar R.
El Cap
Gilbana

El Qantara

El Salhiya
El Ballah

Abu Kebir
Faqus
El Firdan

E G Y P T

El Qassasin
Ismailiya
Lake Timsah

S I N A I

El Tel-el-Kebir
Abu Suweir
← *Suez Canal*

(UNITED ARAB REPUBLIC)

Great Bitter Lake

Fanara
Fayid
Kabrit
Little Bitter Lake

El Ribeiqi
Gineifa

El Shallufa
← *Suez Canal*

El Agrud
El Kubri
Mitla Pass

Suez
El Shatt

Port Taufiq

Uyun Musa
Adabiya

Gulf of Suez
Sudr

Oil Pipelines •—•   Refineries
Railroads +—+   Oil Fields

|||| *Areas occupied by Israel since 10 June 1967.*

Miles 0 ——— 10 ——— 20
Kilometers 0 — 10 — 20 — 30

had been at war, as the Arab states contended, such a state of war must auto-matically have been superseded by their United Nations membership.[26]

Finally, Israel has alleged, the armistice agreement between Egypt and Israel (February 24, 1949) prohibited hostile acts. As a corollary, the armistice termi-nated not only war in the military sense, but also the state of war. As stated by an Israeli jurist, the 1949 agreement was intended to achieve four aims:

(1) To facilitate the transition from truce to permanent peace and bring all hostilities to an end.

(2) To fulfill the obligation of the Security Council to act with respect to threats to the peace, breaches of the peace, and acts of aggression.

(3) To delineate permanent demarcation lines beyond which the armed forces of the respective parties should not move.

(4) To provide for the withdrawal and reduction of armed forces in order to insure the maintenance of the armistice during the transition to permanent peace.[27]

These aims, intended to establish eventual peace between Egypt and Israel, were endorsed by United Nations resolutions of 1949 and 1951 which explicitly called upon Egypt to open the Suez Canal to Israel. Egypt's persistent refusal to open the canal has been regarded by Israel as a violation of the armistice agreement and these United Nations resolutions.

The Egyptian Position. Egypt has denied any violation of international law in refusing free passage to Israel. In the first place, Israel's argument based on general principles of international law takes it for granted that the Suez Canal is an international waterway analogous to an international strait. Egypt has contend-ed that there is a distinction: straits, as natural waterways, have existed from time immemorial, while canals are artificial constructions. Before a canal is built, its territory must fall under the control of some state sovereignty, and the sovereign power must give consent to passage in some form. If the sovereign grants the right of free passage by an express declaration or by an obligation undertaken pursuant to a treaty or other international agreement, it is that sovereign act which entitles other nations to enjoy free passage, rather than any geographical analogy with natural waterways.[28]

Accordingly, the Egyptians have taken the view that it is the Constantinople Convention of 1888, not general principles of international law, that regulates the rights of passage by other nations. If Israel possesses any right to enjoy free passage, such right must derive from this convention. But the convention merely confirmed the right of free passage already recognized by the Ottoman Porte

---

[26] See discussion in Chapter II, *supra*. See also Hans Kelsen, *The Law of the United Nations* (1950), p. 69.

[27] Shabtai Rosenne, *Israel's Armistice Agreements with the Arab States* (Tel Aviv, 1951), p. 33.

[28] "Unlike international rivers and straits, which are natural waterways, international canals are artificially constructed. This essentially differentiating factor has been overlooked by a number of writers who, misled by the similarity of regimes to which both international canals as well as rivers and straits are subject, have tried to find, by an analogy to the latter, a geographical or physical criterion which serves to define an international canal." Joseph A. Obeita, *The International Status of the Suez Canal* (The Hague, 1960), p. 24.

before 1888; it extended to convention signatories such rights in time of war as in time of peace. At the time of signature, other nations were invited to adhere to the convention, but none did so (and Israel never has). But leaving aside for the moment the much-debated question of the rights of nonsignatory third parties, it may be argued that Israel is in a rather special position as a successor state, once a part of the Ottoman Empire. Would not Israel, like Egypt, be entitled to special rights as a successor state?

There is no question that Egypt, specifically mentioned in the Constantinople Convention, was granted special rights as the country immediately connected with the Suez Canal, and certain obligations were imposed upon it.[29] Egypt, as a successor state, according to the general principles of international law, had to accept the obligations already undertaken by the former sovereign, the Ottoman Empire. And, in fact, Egypt on more than one occasion since achieving independence has affirmed its acceptance of the convention obligations.[30] Similarly, Israel, if somehow it can be deemed to have "adhered" to the convention as a matter of law by virtue of its status as a successor state, acquired obligations as well as rights. The Egyptians have pointed out that such obligations required among other things that the Suez Canal remain neutral and not be involved as an area in which war was being waged, nor should it be subject to blockade. Israel, according to Egypt, has not only never indicated its acceptance of such obligations, but in fact has obviously ignored them in carrying its 1967 military operations to the eastern bank of the canal, which it proceeded to fortify.

Egypt more recently appeared to be prepared to concede that if Israel were not involved in a war with Egypt—a war in which Egypt closed the Suez Canal as a defensive measure—Israel would be entitled to the right of free passage. However, Israel's attack on Egyptian territory in June 1967, which Egypt considers to have been an attempt to settle a dispute by force rather than by peaceful methods as required under the United Nations Charter, was regarded as an act of war which justified Egypt's position concerning the security of the canal, especially inasmuch as Israel was not a signatory to the Constantinople Convention. As a third-party beneficiary Israel might theoretically have certain rights under some circumstances.[31] But in a war which Israel allegedly initiated, Egypt claimed that it was justified in closing the canal as a measure of self-defense, not only by

---

[29] . . . "In any circumstance threatening the security and free passage of the Canal, . . . [the agents in Egypt of the treaty powers] shall meet . . . to make the necessary verifications. They shall inform the Khedival Government of the danger perceived, in order that it may take proper steps to assure the protection and the free use of the Canal. . . . They shall demand, in particular, the removal of any work or the dispersion of any assemblage on either bank of the Canal, the purpose or effect of which might be to interfere with the freedom and complete safety of navigation." (Article 8.)

"The Egyptian Government shall, within the limits of its powers based on the Firmans, and under the conditions provided for in the present Treaty, take the necessary measures for enforcing the execution of the said Treaty. In case the Egyptian Government should not have sufficient means at its disposal, it shall appeal to the Imperial Ottoman Government, which shall take the necessary measures for responding to such appeal. . . ." (Article 9.)

[30] See numerous references cited in Majid Khadduri, "Closure of the Suez Canal to Israeli Shipping," *Law and Contemporary Problems,* vol. 33 (1968), at p. 153, n. 23.

[31] See Lord McNair, *Law of Treaties* (1961), pp. 309-21; *Harvard Research in International Law: Law of Treaties* (J. Garner, ed., 1935), p. 924.

general law (U.N. Charter, Article 51), but also by the very provisions of the 1888 convention giving Egypt the responsibility for taking measures to prohibit any state from conducting war in the Canal Zone.[32]

The vexed question of the existence of a state of war between Israel and the Arab states has been considered above in Chapter II. But even if Egypt were to concede that a state of war had not existed prior to June 5, 1967, its determination to keep the Suez Canal closed to Israeli shipping thereafter might find juridical support as a measure necessary for self-defense against sudden attack, on the ground that the closure of the canal to a nonsignatory to the convention falls within Egypt's sovereign prerogatives.

To what extent have Egypt's obligations under the Constantinople Convention restricted its sovereignty over the canal? While never denying its obligations under the convention, Egypt has maintained that it has not violated Article I concerning "free passage" because the measures taken in time of war were "reasonable and necessary measures" for defense purposes, a position supported by a ruling of the Prize Court of Alexandria in 1950.[33] It has been argued, on the other hand, that even "reasonable" and "necessary" measures are forbidden under the convention, Articles 10 and 11 of which can be interpreted as denying Egypt the freedom to take action, even for the defense of its own territory, that might interfere with the free use of the canal.[34] (In this connection reliance has been placed on an opinion of the Permanent Court of International Justice in the *Wimbledon* case,[35] upholding the principle that the canal should remain permanently free as an international waterway.) From Egypt's standpoint, such an interpretation of limitations on its sovereignty when national survival may be at stake is naturally regarded as onerous.

Egypt's assertion of its right to restrict the canal to Israeli shipping in time of war has raised the question whether it can legitimately close the canal during war to other nations, including powers signatory to the 1888 convention. As mentioned above, Egypt denied free passage to Israel on the basis of its inherent right of self-defense.[36] This right, one of the most well established principles of international law, was presumably taken for granted by the parties to the convention as an essential attribute of sovereignty. Article 11 appears to restrict this right, but it seems unreasonable to take the position that Egypt is bound by the convention *in toto*, regardless of whether Israel has accepted the convention's obligations. This would, in effect, impose an international servitude over Egypt for the sake of granting Israel the right of free passage in time of peace or war, while denying

---

[32] The Ottomans appear to have adopted this position after 1888. See Obeita, *Status of the Suez*, pp. 79-87.

[33] *The Flying Trader* (1950), Ann. Dig. 440, 446-447; *Revue Egyptien de Droit International*, vol. 7 (1951), p. 127.

[34] "Similarly, the provisions of Articles IV, V, VI, and VII shall not interfere with the measures which His Majesty the Sultan and His Highness the Khedive . . . might find it necessary to take for securing by their own forces the defence of Egypt and the maintenance of public order. . . ." (Article 10.) "The measures which shall be taken in the cases provided for by Articles IX and X of the present Treaty shall not interfere with the free use of the Canal." (Article 11.)

[35] Permanent Court of International Justice, Series A, no. 1 (1923).

[36] See Richard R. Baxter, "Passage of Ships Through International Waterways in Time of War," *British Year Book of International Law*, vol. 31 (1954), p. 208.

Egypt the right of self-defense. Such an interpretation of the convention would appear to interfere with general principles of international law allowing Egypt to repudiate restrictive measures on its sovereignty imposed without its consent. (Incidentally, it seems unlikely that the Ottoman Porte would have signed the convention subject to any such servitude, inasmuch as it had consistently declared before 1888 that its sovereign control over the canal was not to be impaired by throwing the canal open to other nations.)[37]

Most international lawyers would submit that Egypt has an obligation (which it appears to have acknowledged) to keep the canal open in time of peace to all nations, including Israel, as long as Egypt's security is not involved. However, to the extent that Israel relies on the 1888 convention in demanding a right of free passage, and such a right in and of itself constitutes a threat to Egypt's security as Egypt views its security, it seems unlikely that Egypt would concede that Israel can legitimately invoke one article of the convention (Article 1) while denying Egypt's right to invoke another (Article 10).

After Egypt nationalized the Suez Canal Company in 1956 the United Nations Security Council passed a six-point resolution (October 13, 1956) in which it affirmed that any settlement of the canal question should, *inter alia*, meet the following requirements: (1) free and open transit through the canal, and (2) respect for Egypt's sovereignty.[38] A similar balance is displayed in the Security Council's Resolution 242 of November 22, 1967 (see Chapter II for text). Egyptians would maintain that Egypt's "sovereignty" includes the right to close the canal as a *bona fide* measure of self-defense; Israel, on the other hand, should benefit from the principle of internationality from the moment it ceases to present a threat to Egypt's security.

A Possible Approach to Solution. Egypt has many times reaffirmed its acceptance of the obligations of the convention of 1888 and its respect for the principle of free navigation. Egypt has also declared that any dispute or disagreements which might arise with respect to the convention should be settled in accordance with the Charter of the United Nations, and has suggested that disputes under the convention should be referred to the International Court of Justice. In a letter of July 18, 1957, to the secretary-general, Egypt accepted the compulsory jurisdiction of the international court in all legal disputes that might arise from the application of the convention of 1888.[39] Israel's claim to the right of free passage through the canal may well be an appropriate case to be brought before the court for adjudication; such action might, indeed, constitute a constructive precedent as a means of solving other Arab-Israeli issues on the basis of law and order rather than force or political pressure.[40]

---

[37] Obeita, *Status of the Suez,* pp. 79-87.

[38] Security Council Resolution 118.

[39] *International Court of Justice Year Book, 1956-1957,* pp. 213-14, 241. Cf. U.N. Doc. S/3818/Add. 1 (1957).

[40] A state that supported the 1951 Security Council resolution calling on Egypt to open the Canal to Israeli shipping might (either voluntarily or on Israel's request) invoke the Court's jurisdiction, which "comprises all cases which the parties refer to it and all matters specially provided for in the Charter of the United Nations or in treaties and conventions in force." (Statute of the International Court of Justice, Article 36 [1].)

The Straits of Tiran and the Gulf of Aqaba

In a sense, Sharm al-Shaikh, the military post guarding the Straits of Tiran which command the Gulf of Aqaba, was to the June war of 1967 what Sarajevo was to World War I: a point of no return. Once Egypt, on May 18, 1967, had requested (with unquestioned legality) withdrawal of the United Nations Emergency Force (UNEF) from that position on Egyptian territory and the secretary-general had very promptly acceded to this request (as he felt legally obliged to do), war inexorably followed.

The Israeli case for free navigation of these waters has been developed with skill and force in the United Nations and elsewhere, perhaps nowhere more effectively than by Professor Leo Gross, whose detailed analysis concludes with the opinion that "none of the propositions advanced by the United Arab Republic and its supporters can be accepted as juridically persuasive: neither the claim that the Gulf of Aqaba has been from time immemorial an historic gulf, . . . nor the claim that Israel's territory does not comprise a stretch of the coast of the Gulf, neither the existence of belligerent rights and of a continuing state of war, nor the claim that the Strait of Tiran is not an international waterway." [41]

Yet the claims which Professor Gross dismisses so unequivocally have been made with evident sincerity and have achieved considerable support among jurists of the community of nations, not just in the Arab countries (though they have received but little attention in the U.S.). For a better understanding of current issues in the Middle East, it is therefore worth examining these claims and the rationale behind them. A bit of historical background is an essential part of the analysis.

Background to 1949. It is interesting to note that the littoral positions of some of the states possessing coastlines on the Gulf of Aqaba, especially Israel, have been attained by force. British power was the principal factor in the fixing of the 1906 demarcation line between Egyptian Sinai and the territory controlled by the Ottoman Empire to the east. The line exacted by Britain from the sultan which in 1906 was only an administrative boundary in the legal sense since Egypt was still theoretically under Ottoman sovereignty, later became the international frontier between Egypt and Palestine. Transjordanian and British armored cars secured the Aqaba-Ma'an area for Transjordan in July 1925. The expulsion of Hashimi rulers from the Hijaz brought the Saudi Arabian frontier to the Gulf of Aqaba in December 1925.

Thus the status of the territories controlled by the Arab states on the littoral of the Gulf of Aqaba was established by occupation over a period of time, and not by contractual arrangement. Israel's access to the Gulf of Aqaba was, of course, achieved only recently and under military circumstances. The events whereby Israel established a coastline on the gulf in 1949 are of particular importance to an understanding of Arab attitudes toward developments in the gulf since that time.

---

[41] Leo Gross, "Passage Through the Strait of Tiran and in the Gulf of Aqaba," *Law and Contemporary Problems,* vol. 33 (1968), pp. 125-46, at p. 144.

SUEZ CANAL AND AQABA

In the opening phase of the 1948 war, the Egyptians advanced to a point within 20 miles of Tel Aviv, and through Beersheba to Hebron and Bethlehem. The Egyptians continued to hold southern Palestine until the winter of 1948. On July 15, 1948, the Security Council ordered the parties fighting in Palestine to issue cease-fire orders and refrain from future military action. In the same resolution, the Security Council declared, subject to further decision, that the truce was to remain in force until a peaceful adjustment of the situation was worked out.[42] Pursuant to the July 15 resolution, the Security Council decided on August 19, 1948, that:

> No party is permitted to violate the Truce on the ground that it is undertaking reprisals or retaliations against the other party.

---

[42] S/902, in *U.N. Security Council Documents S/881-1010* (1948).

No party is entitled to gain military or political advantage through violation of the Truce.[43]

Heavy fighting broke out in the Negev in October 1948, and the results were very favorable for Israel. Israeli forces took Beersheba, pushing the Egyptians back to Gaza, and opened the way for a last thrust to secure the rest of the Negev. The remnant of the Egyptian front in Palestine proved to be indefensible.

When hostilities erupted in October, acting mediator Ralph Bunche made a report to the U.N. secretary-general in which he observed: "A serious breach of the truce is involved in the Negev outbreak. . . the military action of the last few days has been on a scale which could only be undertaken after considerable preparation, and could scarcely be explained as simple retaliatory action." [44] But even if Israel's campaign of October 1948 could have been "explained as simple retaliatory action," these operations were still at variance with the August 19, 1948 Security Council Resolution quoted above, and in the Arab view constituted a clear violation thereof.[45]

In another resolution on November 4, 1948, the Security Council called for withdrawal of forces which had advanced beyond the positions held on October 14, and authorized the acting mediator to establish provisional lines beyond which no movement of troops was to take place. (Paragraph 5(1)). This resolution also called upon the parties to negotiate permanent truce lines; failing such agreement, the acting mediator was to establish such permanent lines.[46] Israel's forces did not return to their former positions. Renewed military action took place in December, in response to which the Security Council on December 29, 1948, adopted a resolution calling upon the governments concerned to "implement without further delay the resolution of 4 November and the instructions issued by the Acting Mediator in accordance with paragraph 5 (1) of that resolution." [47]

In a cablegram dated 25 December from the Acting Mediator Ralph Bunche to the president of the Security Council transmitting a report concerning the Negev fighting, Dr. Bunche mentioned that General Riley, chief of staff of the United Nations Truce Supervision Organization, had informed him that "Israeli mobile forces had not been returned to the Negev settlements, that their forces had not been withdrawn from localities occupied since 14 October. . . ." [48]

Israel described the December campaign as a retaliatory action.[49] Following

---

[43] S/983, ibid.

[44] S/1042, *U.N. Security Council Documents S/1011-1099* (1948), p. 6.

[45] Ibid. The "Background of the Outbreak" described in this document seems to confirm that Israel was not retaliating but was applying military power to drive the Egyptians out of Palestine. For secondary sources substantiating this view, see Harry Sacher's *Israel: The Establishment of a State,* Kimche's *Seven Fallen Pillars,* and O'Ballance's *1948 War.*

[46] Document S/1070, ibid.

[47] S/1169, *U.N. Security Council Documents S/1100-1172* (1948).

[48] S/1152, December 27, 1948, in ibid., p. 4.

[49] See ibid. The situation at al-Faluja, where an Egyptian-Sudanese force was surrounded, provided the spark that ignited the outburst of fighting in December 1948. In spite of the fact that the U.N. representative repeatedly stressed that the "truce cannot be exploited as a means of laying siege," "food and medical supplies had not been permitted through Israeli lines to the encircled Egyptians." Nor were the Egyptians permitted to withdraw in compliance with the U.N. plan of November 13 (pp. 3-4). Some observers have speculated that the Egyptians were goaded into an attempt to relieve al-Faluja, an act which was then used by the Israelis to justify their December campaign.

the Security Council's call for a cease-fire and troop withdrawal on December 29, the Egyptians requested a cease-fire and armistice negotiations. The conclusion of the General Armistice Agreement of February 1949 between Egypt and Israel left only Transjordan's Arab Legion between the Israelis and the Gulf of Aqaba. When the Egyptians were defeated, the Arab Legion occupied a line north of the Gulf of Aqaba between Sinai and southern Transjordan. After the beginning of the Jordan-Israel armistice negotiations but before the conclusion of an armistice agreement, Israel advanced toward the gulf and, after some skirmishing, reached it on March 10, 1949.

These facts lay the groundwork for the Arab argument that the Israeli victories of October-December 1948, which crushed the Egyptian position in southern Palestine, were obtained in violation of the Security Council resolutions of August 19 and November 4, 1948; that the Israeli position in the Negev was consolidated despite the instructions of the acting mediator and the Security Council resolution of December 29, 1948; and that Israel's military success in this period, instead of promoting "progress toward implementation of the resolution of the Security Council of 16 November," [50] actually had the opposite effect. Egypt's inability to withstand the attacks of Israel forced the Egyptian government to participate in the negotiations which led to the February 1949 Egypt-Israel Armistice Agreement.

Although the military positions of February 1949 had been attained in violation of Security Council directives, they were recognized by the Egypt-Israel Armistice Agreement and also approved by the United Nations. Article 4 of the agreement stipulated that:

> The basic purposes and spirit of the Armistice would not be served by restoration of previously held military positions, changes from those now held other than as specifically provided for in this Agreement, or by the advance of military forces of either side beyond positions held at the time this Armistice Agreement is signed.[51]

Article 4 also reiterated the principle that no military or political advantage should be gained under the truce ordered by the Security Council, an echo of the Security Council resolution of August 19, 1948.

Although Israeli forces did advance beyond positions held at the time the Egypt-Israel Armistice Agreement was signed, Article 4 applied only to changes of the military positions of Egypt and Israel vis-à-vis one another. Thus, Article 4 operated, like Article 7,[52] to freeze the military situation on the western (Egypt-Israel) front, but it did not limit Israel's freedom of action on the eastern (Transjordan-Israel) front. Nevertheless, Israel was not legally free to move in

---

[50] In S/1152 Dr. Bunche used this phrase to describe the attitude assumed by the Israeli authorities regarding the situation at al-Faluja.

[51] Text in Hurewitz, *Diplomacy*, vol. II, pp. 299-304; *Security Council Official Records—4th Year, Special Supplement No. 3* (Document S/1264/Rev. 1), p. 3.

[52] Article 7 provided that only defensive forces were to be maintained on the western front, but stated that the Egypt-Israel Armistice Agreement's provisions relating to the reduction and withdrawal of forces were not to apply to the eastern front, thus allowing Israel to turn her attention to the front facing the Arab Legion.

that area without restrictions, since the U.N. resolutions cited above were still in effect.

The armistice between Jordan and Israel (April 1949) established a demarcation line "from a point on the Dead Sea to the southernmost tip of Palestine," which was determined by a survey of military positions existing in March 1949. This line, which touched the Gulf of Aqaba east of Um Rashrash (near Elath or Eilat), while not an authoritative boundary, did serve as recognition of Israel's de facto control of the territory west of the line.

Israel's establishment of a position on the Gulf of Aqaba was a *fait accompli,* unlike the entrenchment of Egyptian, Jordanian, and Saudi authority on the shores of the gulf, as successor states of the Ottoman Empire. The United Nations, however, complicated the situation by adding legal and political dimensions to the conflict over the southern Negev in 1948-49. Although the partition plan had given to the Jewish state the southern Negev and an outlet on the Gulf of Aqaba, Count Bernadotte had recommended in the autumn of 1948 that the Negev be placed under an Arab government. The Bernadotte Plan was defeated at the United Nations while the Negev was being forcefully occupied by Israel.

Most Arabs would probably recognize the practical futility of contesting Israel's control of a portion of the coast of the Gulf of Aqaba on the ground that the attainment of that control was inconsistent with U.N. recommendations and "orders." These U.N. actions, although possessed of a legal character, were based largely on political considerations and were overridden by subsequent military developments. Nevertheless, the fact that Israel was able to establish a position on the gulf by force insured that, as far as the Arabs were concerned, the central factor affecting the "rights" of the Aqaba littoral states in the future would be the use of force. From this standpoint, Egyptian restrictions on shipping through the gulf from 1949 to 1956, Israel's opening of the gulf in 1956, the injection of the U.N. presence, the attempted reinstitution of the Egyptian blockade in 1967, and Israel's subsequent seizure of Sinai including the western shore of the gulf, are merely sequential episodes in a continuing struggle for control of the Gulf of Aqaba.

After the arrival of Israel's forces in March 1949, the Arab states on the littoral of the gulf made it clear that they viewed the Israeli presence as a threat to their own interests and rights there. It is in this context that Egypt occupied Tiran and the Sanafir Islands at the mouth of the Gulf of Aqaba in February 1950; the Arab Legion attempted in November-December 1950 to block the main Israeli route to Eilat;[53] Saudi Arabia warned in March 1953 that measures would be taken against planes flying over Saudi territory to and from Israel; the Saudis protested in 1957 against Israel's naval activity in the gulf; and, of course, the Egyptians attempted forcibly to stop shipping bound for Eilat. Jordan and Saudi Arabia were in no position to resist effectively Israel's development of a trade route through the Gulf of Aqaba. Egypt, although it tried, was similarly unable to do so. The result of Egypt's expansion of her blockade to include the Strait of Tiran was

---

[53] Fighting occurred in the Negev in late 1950 when the Arab Legion blocked the main road leading to Eilat. The road was re-opened by Israel forces. In February 1951, Israel and Jordan reached agreement on this matter in the Israel-Jordan Mixed Armistice Commission.

Israel's decision to use force to open the gulf. The analogy of the scorpion and tarantula in a bottle characterized the relationship of Israel and its neighbors on the Gulf of Aqaba from 1949 on.

Assuming the existence of a state of war between Egypt and Israel, as Egypt has claimed, and in the context of the seizure of ships and confiscation of their cargoes which occurred even before the 1956 Sinai campaign, the Egyptian closure of the Gulf of Aqaba could be justified as a legitimate act of war. It will be recalled that it was not just Israel-connected shipping that was being harassed; Israel undertook similar action in the early 1950s such as the confiscation on December 7, 1951, of a cargo of ammunition consigned to the Egyptian Air Force from the French vessel *Champollion* and the seizure on April 25, 1952, of telephone equipment from the Swedish ship *Britta* on the grounds that the equipment was intended for the Syrian army.

Blockade in International Law. Since the Egyptian measures characterized by the term "blockade" were not dealt with by the Egypt-Israel Armistice Agreement, Egypt regarded continuation of the blockade as legitimate. Maintenance of a naval blockade, with its practices of visit and search, seizure of contraband, and regulation of neutral shipping is a right which, if not precluded by specific agreement, can be legitimately exercised as long as a condition of belligerency prevails. Although a blockade may be continued after conclusion of an armistice agreement, there can be no initiation of a blockade which was not in effect during the fighting, on the ground that no political or military advantage should be gained during an armistice.

There was no blockade of the Gulf of Aqaba before the conclusion of the Egypt-Israel Armistice Agreement. On the other hand, there was no shipping to or from Israel through the Gulf of Aqaba until March 1949, when Israel became established on the gulf. Since the gulf was outside the arena of hostilities during the 1948 war, the expansion of the Egyptian blockade to the Strait of Tiran can be rationalized as an attempt to maintain the status quo of the armistice regime, which reflected the political and military situation prior to Israel's move to the gulf. Similarly, the Egyptian attempt to place restrictions on passage through the Strait of Tiran in May 1967 can be regarded as an effort to reestablish the situation which had prevailed in the gulf before Israel's successful resort to force and opening of the gulf in November 1956.

Egypt's institution of the blockade of the Gulf of Aqaba was not a direct measure aimed at Israel's armed forces or population; instead, it was directed against Israel's economy. Closure of the gulf seems in retrospect to have been primarily a political act designed to strengthen Egypt's domestic and diplomatic posture. Nevertheless, from the legal standpoint the blockade was an act of belligerency: economic warfare supported by the threat and use of force. The exercise of coastal control over adjacent waters in a situation of belligerency to advance the policies of the coastal state, even if legitimate in law, obviously cannot be expected to go unopposed by the coastal state's antagonist. Viewed in this light, Israel's right to resist closure of the Gulf of Aqaba was a prerogative derived from the law of war, not an exercise of the right of free and innocent passage. Israel's Sinai campaign of 1956 was patently a violation of her legal obligations undertaken in the 1949 Armistice Agreement. The armistice did not prohibit blockade; it did prohibit the use of military or paramilitary force against the forces or population of the other party. The Arabs may therefore argue that the technical onus of violating the armistice as it applied to the Gulf of Aqaba devolved on Israel.

Innocent Passage. The right of innocent passage through territorial waters is an expression of the general interest of the nations of the world in the use of individual states' waters for peaceful transportation and communication. Against this right must be weighed the interest of coastal states in exercising authority over territorial waters for various purposes, the most important of which is national security. Neither freedom of access to the territorial waters of other states nor the denial of that access is an absolute right, and the right of passage does not inevitably override the right of coastal states to protect their interests by measures taken in their territorial waters. As stated by McDougal and Burke, "While there is no general, arbitrary competence to deny all passage through the territorial sea, there is an occasional exclusive competence which can be exercised for a specified cause." [54] A coastal state may prohibit passage if passage either causes injury or arouses reasonable expectation of harm to a significant coastal interest. McDougal and Burke [55] challenge Leo Gross's assertion that the burden is on the coastal state to show that the act of passage rather than the ship's nature, destination, cargo, or purpose *prejudiced the coastal state*.[56] Coastal states retain the competence to consider factors such as the purpose of passage and the vessel's cargo and destination, as well as acts performed in the territorial sea, in reaching a decision regarding the innocence or noninnocence of passage.[57] The text adopted by the 1958 Geneva Conference on the Law of the Sea and embodied in Article 14, paragraph 4, of the Convention on the Territorial Sea was a modification of the 1956 International Law Commission Report which conformed to Professor Gross's view. The 1958 convention dropped the reference to *acts committed* in the territorial sea, thus making innocence of passage dependent upon a number of factors collateral to the simple act of passage.

In weighing the competing claims of states regarding use of territorial waters, the relationship of the states is of great significance. In fact, the concept of innocent passage in its peacetime context is inappropriate in a wartime situation. Passage by one belligerent's vessels through the territorial waters of its enemy could hardly fail to be an act prejudicial to the interests of the other party. There would seem to be no innocent passage in circumstances in which the interests of one antagonist are harmed if those of his opponent are advanced, and in which the interest of one party in securing transit gives rise to an opposing interest of his

---

[54] Myres Smith McDougal and William T. Burke, *The Public Order of the Oceans* (New Haven, 1962), p. 188.

[55] Ibid., p. 258, n. 221.

[56] Leo Gross, "The Geneva Conference on the Law of the Sea and the Right of Innocent Passage Through the Gulf of Aqaba," *American Journal of International Law,* vol. 53 (1959), p. 582.

[57] McDougal and Burke, *Public Order of Oceans*, p. 258.

enemy in preventing passage. Innocent passage is a function of normal,[58] peaceful *navigational circumstances* when transit does not harm the coastal state. Belligerents cannot rely upon rights which legally and logically exist only during time of peace.

Even when a coastal state is not involved in hostilities, it may deny passage through a strait or other portions of its territorial waters when such passage adversely affects the important interests of that state. As McDougal and Burke write with respect to the application of the right of innocent passage in time of peace:

> . . . the right of innocent passage is thus claimable . . . only if it . . . has no prejudicial effects on coastal security and other consequential interests. If coastal interests are threatened, or actively prejudiced, the coastal state is universally regarded as having the competence to take protective action, including that of prohibiting passage.[59]

In time of war the coastal state's prerogatives are even more comprehensive than in time of peace. In peacetime, the competence of the coastal state to deny passage through its territorial waters is essentially defensive; the raison d'être is the state's right to protect itself from harm or prejudice resulting from the use of its territorial sea. In time of war, the restrictions implied by the term "defensive" are removed and the territorial power may seek to use its control of a strait or other territorial waters to advance its overall position vis-à-vis its enemy (as the Arabs consider Israel to be). While the protection of military security in both war and peace justifies exclusion of passage on the part of the coastal state, the same interest in time of war likewise justifies the use of force by that state's enemy (in this case Israel) in resisting the coastal state's application of its power in its territorial sea.

The same reasoning applies to the attempted reinstitution of blockade measures in the Straits of Tiran in May 1967. The possibility of a reestablishment of restrictions on shipping was not properly anticipated and hedged against in 1956. Egypt was within its legal rights when it demanded the withdrawal of UNEF in 1967. The vague restraining mechanism designed by Secretary-General Hammarskjold in 1956 proved ineffective in 1967 in checking the drift toward another round of fighting.[60] The United Arab Republic considered that it had the legal capacity not only to demand withdrawal of UNEF, but to again impose restrictions upon shipping bound to and from Israel through the Straits of Tiran and the Gulf

---

[58] The term "normal" as used here refers to the circumstances applying most of the time to navigation in most areas of the world. The word "normal", which has in this sense the connotation "peaceful," is inapplicable to the situation in the Gulf of Aqaba, if one adopts the Egyptian view with regard to belligerency.

[59] McDougal and Burke, *Public Order of Oceans,* pp. 189-90.

[60] Although Egypt retained its freedom of action in regard to ultimate withdrawal of consent to the presence of UNEF in Egyptian territory, under the arrangements worked out in November 1956 between the Egyptian government and Hammarskjold, Egypt did not apparently undertake to allow the General Assembly the opportunity to decide whether UNEF's task had been completed before terminating its consent to the presence of the Emergency Force. Egypt did not wait for a General Assembly pronouncement in this connection. On the other hand; the secretary-general, the General Assembly, and the Advisory Committee on UNEF all failed to insist that the U.N. act in accordance with its prerogatives in this matter.

of Aqaba. By the same token, Israel had an even clearer right to use force to resist Egypt's closure of the gulf in 1967 than it had in November 1956, when the legal regime of the Egypt-Israel Armistice Agreement was still officially in force.

Bab el Mandeb

Bab el Mandeb, the strait between Arabia and Africa which connects the Red Sea with the Gulf of Aden and the Indian Ocean, is divided by Perim Island into two channels. The eastern channel is less than two miles wide with a maximum depth of 96 feet. The western channel, between Perim and the African coast, is over 1,000 feet deep in mid-channel and averages about ten miles in width. The name is from the Arabic, and can be translated as "Gate of Lamentation."

Perim Island, with an area of about five square miles, is now a part of South Yemen (formally, the People's Democratic Republic of Yemen), its inhabitants having opted to retain their political connection with the mainland after Aden attained independence in November 1967.

Achievement of independence by what was formerly Aden Colony and Protectorate, and the withdrawal of British forces from this potentially strategic area, have radically changed the political situation in the region of the straits. Both Yemen (formally, the Republic of Yemen) and South Yemen are in position to control traffic through the Bab, and thus effectively to control the southern approaches to the Suez Canal and the Gulf of Aqaba, referred to in earlier sections. On the western—African—side, the Republic of Somalia has a shoreline on the Gulf of Aden, though not on the Bab el Mandeb itself, where the coast forms part of French Somaliland (known since 1968 as Territoire Français des Afars et des Issas), one of the few remaining European enclaves in the Middle East. Should Somalia succeed ultimately in inducing the French to withdraw, Somalia would presumably enhance its position on the western reaches of the Bab. These three young republics (Yemen, South Yemen, Somalia) have all exhibited radical tendencies. Nations interested in maintaining freedom of navigation through the Red Sea and access to Suez, Tiran, Aqaba and Egypt's projected Sumed (i.e., Suez-Mediterranean) pipeline will follow their actions and policies with a watchful eye.

On the day after the birth of the People's Democratic Republic of Yemen, on December 1, 1967, its president announced that his government's policy would embrace the concepts of socialism, the liberation of Palestine, Arab unity, nonalignment, support for national revolutionary movements, and unification of the Arab people in north and south Yemen. Practical action, of course, may prove to be more restrained. Economic considerations should be a positive factor for South Yemen in encouraging international shipping, since Aden's port facilities— in a state of near-stagnation since the closure of the Suez Canal in 1967—would benefit enormously from a revival of traffic to and from the Red Sea.

To the north, the Republic of Yemen has been relatively tranquil since the ending of the civil war and withdrawal of Egyptian troops in 1967. Perhaps the replacement of British rule by an indigenous government in the neighboring state to the south will be accompanied by continued attention to domestic problems.

BAB EL MANDEB

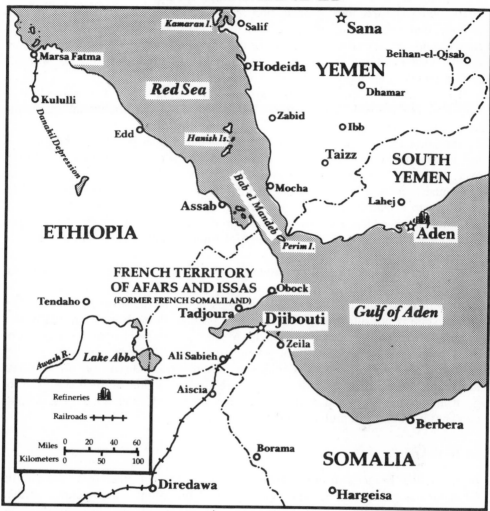

Although the government of the Republic of Yemen espouses ideals similar to those expressed by the leadership of South Yemen, political action seems likely to follow at a distance.

The Somali Republic is in an uneasy relationship with its neighbors of the Horn of Africa. Religious impulses provide a link with Arabs across the Gulf of Aden and elsewhere. Aside from the French enclave, which fuels irredentist and anticolonial sentiment, there has been recurrent tension along Somalia's borders with Ethiopia and Kenya. As in the case of both of the Yemens, Soviet advisers and military assistance have been available.

There has been no indication that the Yemenis or Somalis are disposed to interfere with free passage through the Bab el Mandeb. Since no one claims that there is a "state of war" involving the region, its situation is juridically less contentious than that of the Gulf of Aqaba, the Straits of Tiran, and Suez. Even so, leaving aside the matter of "war" or "peace," it must be observed that in international law freedom of navigation and freedom of overflight are recognized as rights that are absolute only upon and above the high seas. The sovereignty of a state extends to its territorial sea and to the air space over the territorial sea. And an island such as Perim possesses a territorial sea delimited in accordance with the same principles that apply to other land areas.

It is generally accepted that the maximum territorial sea a state may claim is twelve miles, although many nations adhere to the more traditional three-mile limit. Many states do claim twelve miles, and the Geneva Convention on the Territorial Sea and Contiguous Zone of 1958, while it does not define the width, is not inconsistent with the twelve-mile standard (Article 24, paragraph 2). Moreover, Article 12 of the convention provides that where the coasts of two states face each other across a body of water, neither is entitled (failing agreement to the contrary) to extend its territorial sea beyond the median line midway between the baselines from which each state's territorial seas are measured. Assuming a twelve-mile claim on both sides, the Bab el Mandeb falls easily within territorial waters.

While the concept of absolute freedom of the seas does not apply to territorial waters, there is a right of innocent passage through the territorial sea which is enjoyed in peacetime by ships of all states, as noted in the previous section. The coastal state is not allowed to interfere with passage through its territorial waters as long as that passage is not prejudicial to the "peace, good order or security of the coastal state." [61] As has been pointed out above, the principle of innocent passage has been of special significance where straits used for international navigation are concerned, particularly where the navigation of such waters is of great importance for world commerce. So far, fortunately, the "Gate of Lamentation" has not become a problem in this connection.

Shatt al-Arab

In discussing France's frontier difficulties down through the ages, Sanche de Gramont has written: "The odd idea arose that the Rhine was a natural border, whereas the vocation of any river is to be navigated and bridged." [62] This observation applies equally to the Shatt al-Arab, the river formed by the confluence of the Tigris and the Euphrates, and also the smaller Karun, as they meet and flow to the Persian—or Arabian—Gulf.[63] For some fifty miles the Shatt al-Arab constitutes the border between Iraq and Iran. Since 1937 the status of the Shatt has been regulated by a treaty between the two countries, but this treaty was repudiated by Iran in 1969, as will appear in more detail below.

The Shatt is the site of Basra (Iraq's second city after Baghdad) and it is Iraq's chief outlet to the sea, although in recent years the commercial port at Umm Qasr, several miles to the west, has been improved and expanded; and during the 1960s most crude oil shipments from southern Iraqi fields were shifted from Fao on the

---

[61] Geneva Convention on the Territorial Sea and Contiguous Zone (1958), Article 14.
[62] Sanche de Gramont, *The French: Portrait of a People* (New York: Bantam, 1970), p. 6.
[63] The Iranians and most Westerners call it "Persian"; the Arabs tend to insist on "Arabian."

SHATT AL-ARAB

Shatt to a man-made platform some twenty miles offshore in the gulf, known as Khor-el-Amaya. As for Iran, the waterway provides direct access to the refinery at Abadan, to the major commercial port of Khorramshahr (formerly known as Muhammarah), and for the burgeoning industrial complex around Ahwaz. Iran does, however, have other dry-cargo ports along its lengthy coastline (notably Bushire and Bandar Abbas), while over the past decade exports of both crude oil and Abadan's refined products have been largely shifted away from the Shatt, to Kharg Island and Bandar Mashar, respectively. Despite this dispersal, the Shatt remains a major artery for both countries.

Historical Background. The present controversy over the Shatt al-Arab is closely connected with the historic territorial conflicts between the Persian and Ottoman Empires. The various Ottoman-Persian wars beginning in the sixteenth century

89

left the boundaries between the two states undefined. The war of 1821-23 concluded by the Peace Treaty of Erzurum (July 1823), did not in itself settle the frontier, but it did lead to the establishment of a boundary commission in 1843. The work of this commission resulted in the boundary agreement of May 1847, also known as the Treaty of Erzurum. This treaty recognized Persian sovereignty over the port town of Khorramshahr with its anchorage, and over Abadan Island. Otherwise, the treaty gave the Ottomans sovereignty over the entire Shatt up to the left (eastern) bank, but it also provided that "Persian vessels shall have the right to navigate freely without let or hindrance on the Shatt al-Arab from the mouth of the same to the point of contact of the frontiers of the two parties." [64]

On November 4, 1913, as the result of mediation by Britain and Russia, the Ottomans and Persians entered into a protocol providing for the delimitation of the boundary. Article 1 of the protocol provided in part that "the frontier shall follow the course of the Shatt al-Arab as far as the sea, leaving under Ottoman sovereignty the river and all the islands therein," subject to certain exceptions including those mentioned above relating to Khorramshahr and Abadan. The effect of the 1913 protocol was to confirm Ottoman sovereignty up to the low-water mark on the Persian side, subject to the itemized exceptions. A precise and detailed delimitation was made in 1914 by a Boundary Delimitation Commission established pursuant to Article II of the 1913 protocol. [65]

Reference to the League of Nations, 1935. Consistent with these agreements, Iraq established the Basra Port Directorate to supervise navigation of the Shatt. The new Persian regime under Reza Shah, which came to power in the 1920s, was dissatisfied with having Iraq control the waterway, and sought a revision of frontiers by which the boundary would run down the center (or *thalweg*) of the channel. Largely on this account Persia refused diplomatic recognition to Iraq until 1929, and (according to a recently declassified British Naval Intelligence handbook) "openly flouted in many high-handed incidents the authority of the Port Directorate on the Shatt al-Arab." [66]

In a letter dated November 29, 1934, the Iraq government brought the question of its boundary to the attention of the Council of the League of Nations. Essentially the Iraqi position was that, having succeeded the Ottoman Empire, its eastern boundary had been fixed by the Treaty of Erzurum of 1847, the protocol of 1913, and the 1914 delimitation commission. Iraq claimed that Iran had not complied with these arrangements—specifically, in refusing to accept the jurisdiction of the Basra Port Directorate. The Persian government contested the validity of these three agreements. It maintained that the Treaty of Erzurum was invalid because it had not been approved by the Persian government, although it had been ratified by the Persian envoy. It asserted that its envoy had been instructed to sign the

---

[64] See E. Lauterpacht, "River Boundaries: Legal Aspects of the Shatt al-Arab Frontier," *International and Comparative Law Quarterly*, vol. 9 (1960), pp. 208-36, at pp. 209-10. The text of the 1823 treaty appears in Hurewitz, *Diplomacy*, vol. I, pp. 90-92.

[65] Ibid., pp. 211-14.

[66] Naval Intelligence Division, *Iraq and the Persian Gulf* (B.R. 524 [Restricted], Geographical Handbook Series, 1944), p. 317.

treaty before certain Anglo-Russian assurances had been attached to the original agreement. The addition of these "explanations," resulting in the constitution of a new arrangement, was unacceptable to Persia. It was also alleged that the 1913 protocol was invalid because it had not been properly ratified by the Persian parliament (*majlis*), and the 1914 delimitation was void because it was based on an invalid treaty. [67]

The 1937 Treaty and its Repudiation by Iran. The Council of the League appointed a *rapporteur,* an Italian diplomat, and in due course a settlement was reached in a boundary treaty dated July 4, 1937. This treaty was something of a compromise under which Iran accepted the bulk of the Protocol of 1913, while Iraq conceded Iranian sovereignty up to the *thalweg* in the Abadan area, the area of greatest concern to the Iranians in view of rapidly expanding oil export operations there. The preamble of the treaty recited that the king of Iraq and the shah of Iran were "sincerely desirous" of "settling definitively the question of the frontier between their two states." [68]

It is this treaty that the Iranian government repudiated in February 1969, in a statement declaring that Iraq had consistently violated the treaty since its inception and that in any case the treaty "is contrary to all international practices and principles of International Law relating to frontiers"; Iran considered it to be null and void.[69] Specifically, Iran accused Iraq of "completely ignoring for thirty-two years" Article 5 of the 1937 treaty, which stipulated that

> The two . . . Parties . . . undertake to conclude a Convention for the maintenance and improvement of the navigable channel, and for dredging, pilotage, collection of dues, health measures, measures for preventting smuggling, and all other questions concerning navigation through the Shattal-Arab. . . .[70]

Paragraph 2 of the protocol attached to the 1937 treaty provided that Iraq and Iran should conclude a convention in accordance with Article 5 within a year of the entry into force of the treaty, unless this time limit was extended by agreement. It also provided that during this period or any agreed extension thereof, Iraq would retain responsibility for the matters to be settled by the proposed convention.

The convention contemplated by Article 5 of the 1937 treaty never came into being, nor did Iraq and Iran agree on an extension of the time limit as called for by the protocol. As a result, the regime governing the administration of the Shatt al-Arab has never been satisfactorily resolved, as was clearly intended in 1937. In replying to the Iranian allegations in 1969, Iraq did not deny that it had undertaken to enter into a convention, but maintained that

> what actually stood in the way of . . . such agreement was Iran's attitude of trying to turn this [obligation] into a means of claiming

[67] League of Nations, *Official Journal* (February 1935) contains the documents presented by the parties.

[68] "Boundary Treaty Between Iraq and Iran of July 4, 1937," in League of Nations *Treaty Series,* vol. 190 (1938), p. 256.

[69] *Facts about Shatt al-Arab Issue* (Iranian), May 1969, p. 7. Hereinafter cited as "Iranian Facts."

[70] "Treaty Between Iraq and Iran," *supra,* note 68, at p. 257.

rights . . . in the administration of the Shatt al-Arab. This Iran did through alleging the necessity of setting up a Joint Commission for the administration of the Shatt al-Arab.[71]

The Iranian government's position did indeed include the assertion that "Article 5 of the Treaty . . . provides for the joint administration of Shatt al-Arab." [72] Actually, what Article 5 provides is that Iran and Iraq have "a common interest in the navigation of the Shatt al-Arab"; it makes no direct reference to a joint commission or a joint administration. Iraq claimed the right to continue to collect dues and administer navigation pending the conclusion of a convention along the lines called for by Article 5. On the other hand, Iraq had shown no enthusiasm for negotiating a convention which would permit Iran to share in the administration.

The claims of Iraq and Iran regarding the payment of dues are contradictory. Iraq has charged that the Iranians have failed to pay any part of the dues owed by them,[73] while Iran has complained that "Iraq . . . never paid its share of river and harbor maintenance costs." [74] Iran claimed, moreover, that Iraq had used revenues derived from shipping on the Shatt for the construction of facilities such as hotels and an airport at Basra, in violation of Article 4 of the 1937 treaty, which provided that dues should be levied only for costs relating to maintenance of the channel.[75]

Whether or not the Iraqi government's conduct has been of such a nature as to "abrogate the essential clauses" of the 1937 treaty, as Iran has maintained, Iraq's refusal to entertain the Iranian demand for some share in the administration of the Shatt was probably the prime factor leading to the Iranian denunciation of the treaty in 1969 although it has been a long-standing demand. Iraq, it is true, has not used force to assert its rights under the treaty, although it has threatened to do so and has taken action against Iranian fishermen. The Iraqi suggestion that the dispute be referred to the International Court of Justice, assuming it was made in good faith, is evidence of Iraq's preference for peaceful settlement of the dispute. Iran, for its part, has indicated a readiness to negotiate a new treaty with Iraq, either directly or through the good offices of Jordan or Kuwait. Iran has also declared that it is willing to withdraw its troops from the "frontier area" if the Iraqis do the same.[76]

Many of the legal technicalities and arguments presented before the League of Nations in 1935 were superseded by the Treaty of July 1937. However, some of the observations made at that time have continued relevance. First, Iraq maintained that it should have a preferential position regarding the Shatt al-Arab because the Shatt comprised Iraq's only effective access to the sea, while Iran had a long coastline with numerous ports and anchorages on the Persian Gulf. Iran pointed out that Iraq did not need to exercise sovereignty over the entire

71 *Facts Concerning the Iraqi-Iranian Frontier* (Baghdad: Iraqi Ministry of Foreign Affairs, January 1960), p. 20. Hereinafter cited as "Iraqi Facts."

72 *Iranian Facts,* p. 6.

73 *Iraqi Facts,* p. 25.

74 *The Christian Science Monitor,* June 5, 1969, p. 4.

75 Statement by Amir Khosrow Afshar, Deputy Minister of Foreign Affairs of Iran, in the Iranian Senate, April 19, 1969.

76 *Kayhan International* (Teheran), June 7, 1969, p. 2.

waterway in order to maintain access to the sea. From Iran's point of view, a legal regime which gave Iraq exclusive sovereignty over the Shatt al-Arab placed the latter state in a tempting position from which it could interfere with navigation to Abadan and Khorramshahr by acts of omission as well as of commission. For example, the channel might be allowed to fill up on the Iranian side. Although the standard international practice, according to which the *thalweg* forms the boundary line between the territory of two riparian states, does not have effect in situations where a boundary treaty sets forth other provisions, the *thalweg* principle would appear to provide for equitable protection of the interests of both sides in the Shatt al-Arab.

On the other hand, the navigational interests of Iran and Iraq were provided for by the 1937 treaty even though the *thalweg* was not the boundary line except in the Abadan area. Article 4 of the Treaty of 1937 stipulated:

> (a) The Shatt al-Arab shall remain open on equal terms to the trading vessels of all countries. All dues levied shall be . . . for services rendered and shall be devoted exclusively to . . . the cost of upkeep . . . or improvement of the navigable channel and the approach to the Shatt al-Arab.
> (b) The Shatt al-Arab shall remain open for the passage of vessels of war and other vessels of the two . . . Parties not engaged in trade.
> (c) The circumstances that the frontier in the Shatt al-Arab sometimes follows the low water mark and sometimes the *thalweg* or medium filum aquae shall not . . . affect the . . . Parties' right of user along the whole length of the river.[77]

Persia put forth the view in 1935 that a frontier

> is not [an] aggressive line, which constricts the development of one party to the advantage of the other; it is a partitioning line open to the free communications of both the sovereign states . . . it implies the equal use . . . of a property which they must learn, by joint administration, to associate with each other.[78]

Except for the reference to joint administration, this principle of "a partitioning line open to free communications and equal use" regarding the Shatt al-Arab was institutionalized in the 1937 treaty. But the principle of joint administration was not, as noted above, carried out under the treaty.

Another of the assertions of the Persian government, which has been revived in the 1969 controversy, was that

> the Iraqi authorities have always insisted on maintaining their point of view as to the validity of Iraq's titles—titles based on obsolete documents . . . relating to a period when the Persian and Ottoman Empires were under the aggressive influence of foreign Powers and . . . contrary to the requirements of the present time. . . . The Royal (Iraqi) Government . . . persisted in maintaining its point of view without appearing to realize that great changes have occurred in the world. . . .[79]

---

[77] League of Nations, *Treaty Series,* vol. 190 (1938), p. 257.
[78] League of Nations, *Official Journal* (February 1935), p. 122.
[79] Ibid., p. 222.

Against this viewpoint the Iraqi foreign minister stated in 1935 that his government adopted its attitude because the frontier then existing was "the frontier laid down by law" and was the only frontier "certain and fixed in fact." He could not see "what these frontiers can be except the ones laid down in the past, unless and until they are altered by some method recognized by international law." [80]

These divergent views represent almost classic examples of two difficulties which plague efforts at peaceful settlement of international disputes. Frequently, one party to a bilateral treaty wants to retain a legal arrangement which it considers consonant with its national interests while the other party wishes to replace the old regime with another more suitable for its goals and purposes. As international circumstances change, some alteration of legal arrangements often seems appropriate. Yet the need for stability and certainty in international relations militates against acceptance of the validity of unilateral denunciation of treaty obligations without the acquiescence of the other party or parties. There is also a problem regarding "unequal" treaties, entered into with the more or less obvious presence of pressure emanating from a European power. Most often this objection to a treaty is directed by a small state toward an agreement concluded between an "imperialist" state and itself. This complaint of "inequality" has also, however, spilled over into situations where the disengagement of a former colonial state has led to shifts in power relationships. In the case of the controversy over the Shatt al-Arab, both parties accuse each other of trying to benefit from an unfair application of power. Iran objects to the fact that the 1937 treaty "was drawn up to favor Iraq in the days when Britain had a major voice in Iraqi affairs and the British Navy ruled the Persian Gulf." [81] The Iranian deputy minister of foreign affairs has stated that: "the effects and the results emanating from colonialism must . . . vanish. . . . Is it not . . . astonishing . . . that although colonialism has been finished . . . , the Iraqi Government will try with all its might to safeguard the effects and the results of colonialism of which this treaty is a specimen?" [82] Iraq, on the other hand, has complained that Iran "seized the opportunity of the Iraqi Coup of 1936 to exert all possible pressure on the new government of Iraq which was at that time in great need for internal stability and external peace in order to secure a new agreement embodying its ambition in the Shatt al-Arab." [83]

Both disputants object to the fact that power was used to influence unduly the apportionment of rights under the 1937 treaty. As for recent events, Iraq accuses Iran of forcefully overturning a legitimate treaty, while Iran asserts that Iraq has unreasonably resorted to the use and threat of force to prosecute her claims under that treaty.

---

[80] Ibid., pp. 113-17.
[81] *New York Times,* May 19, 1969, p. 2.
[82] See statement of Amir Khosrow Afshar, *supra,* note 75.
[83] *Iraqi Facts.*

V. OTHER TERRITORIAL AND JURISDICTIONAL ISSUES

The foundation of the Islamic state was ideological, not territorial. It has been only recently, under the impact of Western territorial concepts of state and law, that Muslim countries have begun to change traditional concepts of law and polity from personal to territorial.[1] The Islamic state underwent territorial segregation before Western legal concepts were adopted, but the division into separate territorial units led to no recognized legal entities until Western concepts of territorial sovereignty and law were accepted by Muslim sovereigns. Persia and Turkey were territorially separated at the opening of the sixteenth century, but it was not until the mid-19th that they agreed to coexist as separate territorial sovereignties and to accept recognized frontiers separating them. In the interim, Persia and Turkey were compelled to accept territorial adjustments with foreign powers and to define recognized frontiers by contractual arrangements. By the end of World War I, when the last traditionally organized Islamic entity—the Ottoman Empire—disappeared, all the Islamic states of the Middle East emerged as sovereign states and accepted territoriality as the basis for their relationships among themselves and with non-Muslim countries.

Since most Middle Eastern countries have emerged as territorial states comparatively recently, it is not unnatural that several jurisdictional differences should have arisen, relating either to frontiers or to other territorial questions. Some of these issues are quite recent, resulting from the partition of Palestine and the creation of Israel; others of longer standing go back to World War I and even before. Territorial disputes relating to the partition of Palestine have been dealt with in other parts of this work;[2] others, relating to disputed sovereignty, the delineation of frontiers, and the allocation of river waters are discussed in this chapter. A note on the legal aspects of overflight rights is also included.

The Bahrain Islands

Britain's withdrawal of its military presence from the Persian (or Arabian) Gulf in 1971 was preceded by the termination of its special treaty relationship with Kuwait in 1961. This special status—virtually tantamount to a protectorate, though not officially so designated—also applies to Bahrain, Qatar and the Trucial States. With respect to these countries this special status will soon be terminated or at least substantially modified. With Britain's impending relinquishment of its stabilizing role, the smaller states of the Persian Gulf have initiated negotiations with a view to establishing a gulf federation. Britain, recognizing the potential

---

[1] See Chapter I, above. See also, Majid Khadduri, *War and Peace in the Law of Islam* (Baltimore, 1955), Chapter 3.

[2] See Chapters II and III.

95

vacuum that will be created by its withdrawal, seems to be satisfied to play the role of honest broker in quietly encouraging the process of organizing such a federation. There are, however, many obstacles to be overcome. Among the most conspicuous of these is Iran's long-standing claim to sovereignty over Bahrain; for Bahrain would be the most populous, the most advanced, and one of the wealthiest members of the federation. Bahrain's participation might be crucial to the federation's viability. Moreover, the federation will be heavily dependent upon Iranian good will for its success. In short, some sort of resolution of the Iranian claim would contribute substantially toward regional stability in the gulf area.

The term "Bahrain" (which means "two seas") was originally applied to the continental coast of Arabia (al-Hasa), the peninsula of Qatar, and the group of islands that separate the bay between al-Hasa and Qatar into the "two seas." Later this term came to be applied only to those islands which form the "two seas." The Bahrain Islands form an archipelago composed largely of sedimentary rock. The archipelago includes Bahrain itself (the largest, 27 miles long by 10 miles wide), Muharraq (second in size, five miles in length, situated to the north of Bahrain to which it is connected by a causeway), Sitra, Umm Na'san, and a number of smaller islands. The islands were famous in earlier times for their pearl fisheries; they are important now as the location of moderate-sized oil reserves, a large refinery, and as a leading commercial center.[3]

Iran's claim of sovereignty became the occasion for a vigorous exchange of diplomatic correspondence with the British government (and later the United States government) following the discovery of oil in the 1920s and the granting of a concession by the ruler of Bahrain, with Britain's consent, to an American-owned oil company incorporated in Canada.[4] But Iran's claim had been advanced repeatedly in the 19th century, as Britain progressively developed its network of treaties and other arrangements in the gulf. Today the claim is once more relevant in the diplomatic maneuvering connected with the contemplated gulf federation. On what grounds does Iran justify its claim?

The main thrust of Iran's argument may be summarized as follows: there has never existed in the past an independent entity called the State of Bahrain; Persian occupation of the islands was continuous over many centuries (interrupted only by Portuguese occupation from 1507 to 1602); Iran has never ceded sovereignty over Bahrain to any other power, nor has it recognized the ruler of Bahrain as an independent chief of state.[5] Iranian writers have regarded British protec-

---

[3] James H. D. Belgrave, *Welcome to Bahrain,* 4th ed. (Manama, 1960) is an excellent descriptive guidebook. The most generally accepted spelling is now "Bahrain," although "Bahrein" and "Bahrayn" are also sometimes used.

[4] See Fereydoun Adamiyat, *Bahrein Islands: A Legal and Diplomatic Study of the British-Iranian Controversy* (New York: Praeger, 1955), Chapter VI. For the oil concession background, see David H. Finnie, *Desert Enterprise: The Middle East Oil Industry in its Local Environment* (Cambridge: Harvard University Press, 1958), pp. 33-35.

[5] Iran has also argued that Britain itself recognized Iranian sovereignty on various occasions during the nineteenth century, a contention consistently denied by the British. See Adamiyat, *Bahrein Islands,* pp. 212ff; Majid Khadduri, "Iran's Claim to the Sovereignty of Bahrayn," *American Journal of International Law,* vol. 45 (1951), at pp. 634-38; J. C. Hurewitz, *Diplomacy in the Near and Middle East* (Princeton: Van Nostrand, 1956), vol. I, p. 172.

BAHRAIN AND THE PERSIAN GULF STATES

Inset (upper):

BAHRAIN

El Muharraq
Manama
El Buddayyi
Rifa-el-Gharbi
Az Zallaq
Umm Nasan
Sitra
Awali
El Amar
El Hadd
Er Rumaytha
Ras-el-Barr

Main map:

IRAQ

IRAN

Euphrates R.

Abadeh

Shiraz

Kazerun

Jahrom

Galeh Dar

Lar

Bushire

Bandar Abbas

Minab

Strait of Hormuz

Qeshm I.

Qasab

Lavan I.

Davan I.

Ahwaz

Abadan

Kharg I.

Kuwait

KUWAIT

NEUTRAL ZONE

Shubah

Basra

Safaniya

Manifeh

Ras Tanura

Dhahran

BAHRAIN

Manama

QATAR

Doha

Hofuf

Haradh

As Sayh

Shaqra

Riyadh

SAUDI ARABIA

Persian or Arab Gulf

Ras-el-Khaimah

Umm-el-Qaiwain

Ajman

Sharjah

Dubai

Abu Dhabi

TRUCIAL STATES

The Empty Quarter

Fujairah

Sohar

Muscat

Sur

Nazwa

MUSCAT AND OMAN

Gulf of Oman

Arabian Sea

Legend:

Oil Pipelines

Oil Fields

Refineries

Miles   0   50   100   200

Kilometers   0   100   200

97

tion as intervention in the domestic affairs of the islands and hence in the domestic affairs of Iran itself.[6]

Although the early history of Bahrain is obscure, it is known that the islands have been inhabited since prehistoric times.[7] Many foreigners, from the ancient Babylonians to the modern-day British, have controlled them from time to time. The Persians seem to have dominated Bahrain before the rise of Islam in the seventh century, but even before this Arabs had migrated into the Persian Gulf coasts and settled on the islands. The rise of Islam allowed the Arabs to acquire and then to consolidate control of Bahrain. Their domination lasted from the seventh century until the opening of the 16th century, when the islands passed into Portuguese hands.[8] The rule of the Portuguese, which lasted about a century, came to an end when Portugal diverted its forces from the east to be used in Europe, just before Spain annexed Portugal. These circumstances proved favorable for a revival of Persian interests in the gulf.

Persian intervention in the affairs of Bahrain, according to Arab writers, was prompted by conflict between Sunnis and Shi'is, members of the two main Islamic sects, both of which were well established in Bahrain at this time.[9] Tribal chiefs of the two sects in Bahrain had long sought outside help against each other. Just as the Ottoman Empire had become the center of Sunni power, so Persia was looked upon by the Shi'i world as the defender of the Shi'i rights. During the Persian reign of Shah Abbas (1587-1629), a great protagonist of the Shi'i cause, power in Bahrain was in the hands of a Sunni chief. The Shi'is on Bahrain appealed to Persia, and the shah, assisted by the British, then expelled the remaining Portuguese forces from Bahrain in 1602 and from Hormuz in 1622.[10]

From 1602 the Bahrain Islands remained more or less under Persian domination until 1783; but during this period they became the target of attack by neighboring rulers. In 1717 and 1720 the Arab chiefs of Muscat twice attacked the islands and wrested them from Persia. It was not until 1737 that they were restored to Persian rule under Nadir Shah. Persian rule, however, remained unstable, for Nadir Shah's immediate successors became involved in a contest for supremacy over the islands with the chiefs of the Utubi tribes, who were then ruling the coast of Arabia across the bay from Bahrain. The Utubis came originally from Najd and settled in Kuwait, but later, with the help of chiefs of the al-Sabah tribe, which ruled Kuwait, they moved to al-Hasa and established themselves at Zubara, a town situated in the peninsula of Qatar facing the Bahrain Islands.

In 1783 Sheik Ahmad al-Khalifa, then chief of the Utubi tribes and ruler of

---

[6] See Malek Esmaili, *Le Golfe Persique et les Iles de Bahrein* (Paris, 1936); Gholam-Reza Tadjbakhche, *La Question des Iles Bahrein* (Paris, 1960); Adamiyat, *Bahrein Islands.*

[7] For recently published light on the fascinating prehistory of Bahrain and the Gulf in general, see Geoffrey Bibby, *Looking for Dilmun* (New York: Knopf, 1970).

[8] Oestrup gives the date 1507 as the beginning of Portuguese rule (*Encyclopedia of Islam*, vol. I, p. 585), and this seems to be the source of the date given in the Iranian note of August 2, 1928 (League of Nations, *Official Journal*, September 1928, p. 1361).

[9] Al-Nabhani, *Tarikh al-Bahrayn* (Cairo, 1924); Amin al-Rihani, *Muluk al-Arab,* 2nd ed. (Beirut, 1929), vol. II, Chapters 5 and 6.

[10] Other sources give 1622 as the date of Portuguese expulsion from Bahrain. See discussion in Adamiyat, *Bahrein Islands,* p. 217, n. 25.

Zubara, attacked Bahrain and annexed it to his territory; but when Zubara was overrun by the Wahhabi forces a few years later, the Khalifa chiefs moved their seat of government to Bahrain, abandoning their Arabian dominion.

While Bahrain was freed from Persian rule, it never ceased to be a bone of contention among neighboring rulers, such as the sultans of Muscat and the Wahhabi amirs. It was partly owing to this threat from neighboring rulers, but mainly to internal feuding among members of the Khalifa family (chief of the Utubi tribes) that Great Britain found ample reasons for intervention.

In 1820, when Great Britain had already made it appearance in the Persian Gulf, the chiefs of Bahrain sought British support for security from outside attack as well as for internal stability. This coincided with Britain's increasing interests in the security of its trade relations and in the suppression of piracy and the slave trade in the Persian Gulf. Britain signed the first of a series of treaties with the sheiks of Bahrain, which did not encroach upon their independence; but these treaties resulted later in the gradual change of the islands from independent to dependent status.

This brief sketch indicates that Bahrain was able to maintain a large measure of internal independence even when it had fallen under foreign control. Apart from its uncertain status in antiquity, the islands passed under Arab authority at the opening of the seventh century and remained, either as an integral part of the Arab Empire or as a semi-independent entity, until the 16th century. Arab rule, accordingly, may be said to have lasted for more than eight centuries. Portuguese rule lasted for about one century (circa 1507 to 1602), and Persian rule (1602-1783) for a little over one and a half centuries. From a purely historical standpoint, the Persian period left no special racial or cultural impact on the inhabitants of the islands. Contrary to the Iranian contention, the inhabitants of the islands either originally migrated from Arabia or were Arabicized under Arab rule. They speak the Arabic language. Many of them speak Persian too. Their manners and customs are essentially Arabian. Finally, they have been ruled since 1783 by their own Arab chiefs, even though they have acknowledged British protection. Their association with the British has lasted longer than Persian rule.[11]

British Protection. When Napoleon invaded Egypt in 1798, a period of Anglo-French rivalry for the domination of eastern waters began. The Persian Gulf was one portion of the area in which the struggle was fought. When Napoleon had been eliminated, the eastern waters, including the Persian Gulf, became an undisputed field of British influence and commerce. Britain began to prepare the way by combatting piracy and the slave trade, and it signed treaties with Persian Gulf chiefs which within a few years made Britain the paramount power in the gulf area.

A General Treaty for the Pacification of the Persian Gulf, the first of a series which Britain negotiated with the gulf chiefs, was signed on January 8, 1820.[12]

[11] Adamiyat provides a differing historical analysis from a frankly pro-Iranian standpoint.

[12] Text of the treaty appears in C. U. Aitchison, *A Collection of Treaties, Engagements and Sanads Relating to India and the Neighbouring Countries,* 5th ed. (Calcutta, 1933), vol. XI, pp. 245-47; also in Hurewitz, *Diplomacy,* vol. I, pp. 88-90.

The treaty provided that: "There shall be a cessation of plunder and piracy by land and sea on the part of the Arabs, who are parties to this contract, forever" (Article 1); and that:

> If any individual of the people of the Arabs contracting shall attack any that pass by land or sea of any nation whatsoever, in the way of plunder and piracy and not of acknowledged war, he shall be accounted an enemy of all mankind and shall be held to have forfeited both life and goods. An acknowledged war is that which is proclaimed, avowed, and ordered by government against government; and the killing of men and taking of goods without proclamation, avowal, and the order of a government, is plunder and piracy (Article 2).

Article 4 required the Arab chiefs "not to fight with each other" and to maintain peace with the British government; Article 9 prohibited slave trade and prevented the Arabs from carrying slaves in their vessels.

While the general treaty was jointly signed by the Arab gulf chiefs, bilateral agreements were signed for its implementation in each of the chiefs' territories. Bahrain's agreement (February 15, 1820) provided:

> That the Sheiks shall not permit from henceforth, in Bahrein or its dependencies, the sale of any commodities which have been procured by means of plunder and piracy, nor allow their people to sell anything of any kind whatsoever to such persons as may be engaged in the practice of plunder and piracy; and if any of their people shall act contrary hereto, it shall be equivalent to an act of piracy on the part of such individuals (Article 1).[13]

Article 2 required the delivery of all Indian prisoners in Bahrain and Article 3, the final article, stated the adherence of the sheik to the General Pacification Treaty.

There is nothing in this agreement, nor in the General Pacification Treaty, which infringed on the powers or the independence of the sheik of Bahrain. Britain readily recognized the sheik as an independent ruler. When, accordingly, the commander of the Egyptian forces had overrun the interior of Najd in the course of his wars with the Wahhabis, and announced his intention of taking Bahrain as part of Najd, he was informed that the British government could not admit any claim of Egypt to Bahrain. The British government declined to recognize similar claims advanced by Persia on various occasions during the nineteenth century. The Ottoman authorities made overtures to the sheik of Bahrain with the object of obtaining his recognition of the supremacy of the Porte. "The ministers of the Sultan," said Aitchison, "were informed that, as the British government had had treaty relations with Bahrein as an independent power, they could not acknowledge or acquiesce in any arrangement for placing the island under the sovereignty or protection of the Porte." [14]

Rivalry among the members of the Khalifa family during the latter half of the nineteenth century was, perhaps, the principal reason prompting Great Britain to conclude further treaties with the sheiks of Bahrain. As a consequence, there may have been British encroachment on their independence, lest the sheiks should

---

[13] Aitchison, *Collection of Treaties,* p. 233.
[14] Ibid., p. 191.

permit other powers to control the islands. Jealousy among the chiefs prompted Britain to expel the ruler of Bahrain in 1850. Both Turkey and Persia were tempted to exploit this rivalry to their advantage. The sheiks began to play one power off against another, and one of them, Sheik Muhammad Khalifa, claimed the protection of both Turkey and Persia. The Persian flag was hoisted on the arrival of an agent of Persia, only to be pulled down and replaced by the Turkish flag on the arrival of the Turkish agent.

Great Britain made representations to both Turkey and Persia, which resulted in the disappearance of their agents. The sheik's relations with his neighbors, his powers regarding making war, his activities in piracy and the slave trade were all restricted in a treaty which promised British protection from foreign aggression. This treaty (signed on May 31, 1861), stated that the sheik was recognized as an "independent ruler," but virtually reduced the islands to the status of a protectorate. The treaty stated:[15]

> I [the Sheik] agree to abstain from all maritime aggressions of every description, from the prosecution of war, piracy, and slavery by sea, so long as I receive the support of the British Government in the maintenance of the security of my own possessions against similar aggressions directed against them by the chiefs and tribes of this Gulf (Article 2).

And it also provided that:

> In order that the above engagements may be fulfilled I [the Sheik] agree to make known all aggressions and depredations which may be designed, or take place at sea, against myself, territories, or subjects, as early as possible to the British Resident in the Persian Gulf, as the arbitrator in such cases, promising that no act of aggression or retaliation shall be committed at sea by Bahrein or in the name of Bahrein, by myself or others under me, on other tribes, without his consent or that of the British Government, if it should be necessary to procure it. . . .

In 1867 Sheik Muhammad was involved in a struggle with the chief of Qatar, the peninsular area on Arabia's north coast, and with one of the rival chiefs of his family, supported by the Persian government. Britain, while it tried to restrain the sheik from his aggressive designs on Qatar, defended Bahrain's independence against Persia. Thereupon Sheik Muhammad was deposed by Britain and his brother, Ali ibn Khalifa, signed an agreement in which he agreed to abstain from aggression and to appeal to the British resident as arbitrator in any quarrel with his neighbors.[16]

During the latter part of the nineteenth century the Ottoman authorities in Arabia and Iraq made attempts to extend their influence to Bahrain; but both Britain and the sheik of Bahrain protested to the Ottoman Porte that Bahrain was an independent country. In 1880 the ruler of Bahrain, Sheik Isa ibn Ali al-Khalifa, signed an agreement with Great Britain in which he agreed to abstain from negotiations or making treaties with any foreign power without Britain's

---

[15] Ibid., pp. 234-36.
[16] Ibid., pp. 236-37.

consent. The agreement, dated December 22, 1880,[17] consisted of a single article:

> I, Isa ibn Ali al-Khalifeh, Chief of Bahrein, hereby bind myself and successors in the Government of Bahrein to the British Government to abstain from entering into negotiations or making treaties of any sort with any State or Government other than the British without the consent of the said British Government, and to refuse permission to any other Government than the British to establish diplomatic or consular agencies or coaling depots in our territory, unless with the consent of the British Government. . . .

In 1892 this agreement was supplemented by another in which Sheik Isa reluctantly accepted further limitation upon his powers. The material part of the text of the agreement of March 13, 1892, is as follows:[18]

> 1. That I [Sheik Isa] will on no account enter into any agreement on correspondence with any power other than the British Government.
>
> 2. That without the assent of the British Government, I will not consent to the residence within my territory of the agent of any other Government.
>
> 3. That I will on no account accede, sell, mortgage, or otherwise give for occupation any part of my territory save to the British Government.

These two agreements seem to have placed the Bahrain Islands under British protection by the sheik's acceptance of British advice in the conduct of foreign relations. When in the following year, the Ottoman Porte claimed that the people of Bahrain were regarded as Ottoman subjects within Ottoman territories and objected to British officials taking up the cases of Bahrain subjects suffering from piracy, the British government replied that Bahrain was under "British protection."[19]

In 1900 a British political agency, subordinate to the political resident in the Persian Gulf, was established in Bahrain. In 1909 Sheik Isa agreed not to allow the establishment in Bahrain of post offices by any foreign government other than the British. In 1914 Sheik Isa agreed that he would not himself, nor would he allow any foreign interest to, exploit the oil resources of Bahrain without the approval of the British government.[20]

The foregoing treaty relations, often referred to as constituting "protection," touched upon matters beyond those normally covered in treaties between the protecting and the protected states. The sheiks of Bahrain not only gave up some of their powers regarding the conduct of foreign relations—an action which is normal in international practice—but they also relinquished certain aspects of their internal sovereignty which would cast serious doubt as to whether Bahrain is a bona fide protectorate. The status of Bahrain, which constitutes a peculiar juridical position, is difficult to define in terms of modern international law; but this peculiarity raises the very issue whether Bahrain's status, the legacy of various

---

[17] Ibid., p. 237; Hurewitz, *Diplomacy*, vol. I, p. 194.
[18] Aitchison, *Collection of Treaties*, p. 238; Hurewitz, *Diplomacy*, vol. I, p. 209.
[19] Aitchison, *Collection of Treaties*, p. 196.
[20] Text in Abbas Faroughy, *The Bahrein Islands, 750-1951* (New York: 1951), p. 124.

legal transactions made at a time when the Eastern world was outside the pale of international law, should be defined merely in terms of modern juridical rules.

The Juridical Status of Bahrain. Under the general principles of Islamic law the Bahrain Islands, as Muslim territory, are regarded as part of the *dar al-Islam* (territory of Islam) and its ruler must owe allegiance to the Caliph, the supreme head of the Islamic state. The Caliph, who derives his authority from the sacred law, is charged with the functions of maintaining the integrity of *dar al-Islam* and the defense of its people. It follows, accordingly, that so long as there was a Caliph in evidence, all Muslims owed allegiance to him and acknowledged his ultimate authority. The Bahrain Islands, until the time of the abolition of the Caliphate, must be regarded as part of the Caliph's dominions in principle. Even the Persian occupation might be regarded as a continuation of Islamic sovereignty, for the Persian Shah, whether he acknowledged the Caliph's overlordship or ruled as a rival, claimed to fulfill the same functions enjoined by the sacred law over both his country and Bahrain.

Long before the opening of the nineteenth century, when Great Britain made her appearance in the Persian Gulf, the authority of the Caliph had declined and certain portions of his dominions had passed under foreign rule. The occupation of Muslim territories by non-Muslim powers was never recognized by the Caliph and was regarded as an anomaly under Islamic law. It was tolerated only so long as Muslim power was not strong enough to restore those territories to the rule of the sacred law.

The European powers, on their part, when they came into contact with the Islamic world, were confronted with a civilization so different from their own that they found it expedient not to apply their own principles of international law in conducting their relations with Muslims and other Eastern people. In the circumstances, neither would Islam recognize Christian rule in its dominion nor were the European powers prepared at first to regard Eastern lands as falling under the pale of European international law. Thus the European jurists began to justify certain actions or violations of international law in the East, which would never have been tolerated in Europe, on the ground that Eastern lands were never recognized by European nations.[21]

In the case of such dependent territories as Bahrain and other Eastern protectorates, the jurists distinguish between a civilized protectorate of the type recognized by international law and an Eastern "protected state" associated with European power. In the former, the protecting state undertakes the conduct of the smaller or weaker state's external relations, but it is understood that the attributes of the weaker state's internal sovereignty are left intact. In the case of Eastern "protected states" the protecting power, in addition to its right to control foreign relations, is entitled, as stated by the Berlin Conference of 1884-85, to the right of administering justice over subjects of other civilized states, and, by the General Act of the Brussels Conference of 1890, to the right of organizing "the administration,

---

[21] For the application of such considerations in respect of Algeria, see James Lorimer, *Institutes of the Law of Nations* (Edinburgh, 1884), vol. II, pp. 160-61.

judicial, religious and military services in the African territories placed under the sovereignty or protectorate of civilized nations." [22]

Professor Robbins, in his discussion of the juridical status of Aden, used the very convenient term "colonial protectorates," which he applied to Aden and similar Asiatic protectorates. Such territories were administered as part of the British Empire and can hardly be distinguished from colonies. Robbins went on to argue that international law recognized only real, not colonial, protectorates, the latter having no international status.[23] But it is doubtful whether this term is adequate to define the existing status of Bahrain. The ruler of Bahrain is invariably referred to as an independent ruler, and it is said that his country is under British protection (though not a "protectorate"); as a practical matter his sovereign rights have been substantially infringed by the engagements he has entered into with the British. The rulers of Bahrain, like the rulers of Kuwait until 1961, have had full control over local administration, though they have accepted British advice.

After more than a century of controversy over the status of Bahrain, this long-standing dispute between Iran and Great Britain was at last settled in 1970. The eventual withdrawal of British forces from the Gulf in 1971, announced two years earlier, may have induced both Britain and Iran to come to an understanding on the future position of Bahrain. Iran, realizing Bahrain's connections with the coastal Arab states, especially Saudi Arabia, seemed to prefer an independent Bahrain after Britain's withdrawal rather than her dependence on the neighboring Arab states.

Early in 1969 the Shah of Iran declared the renunciation of the use of force for the settlement of the Bahrain controversy and stated that he would accept the wishes of the people of Bahrain to decide the future status of their country. Both Britain and Iran accordingly agreed to bring the matter of determining the wishes of the people of Bahrain to the United Nations. The secretary-general of the United Nations was asked to exercise his good offices and to report to the Security Council the wishes of the people of Bahrain on the strength of a report by a fact-finding commission to be appointed by him. The commission was appointed and dispatched to Bahrain in March 1970. It reported on May 2 that the overwhelming majority of the people wanted independence. The report was circulated to and endorsed by the Security Council on May 11, 1970. Following the council's endorsement, Iran formally renounced her claim to the sovereignty of Bahrain. In 1971 an agreement was signed between Britain and Bahrain by virtue of which Bahrain was recognized as an independent state.

The settlement of this long-standing dispute is another example of the possibility of settling Middle Eastern problems by peaceful rather than by violent methods. Recourse to the United Nations as a medium either to exercise good offices, as in

---

[22] Cf. W. E. Hall, *A Treatise on the Foreign Powers and Jurisdiction of the British Crown* (Oxford, 1895), pp. 204-07.

[23] Robert R. Robbins, "The Legal Status of Aden Colony and the Aden Protectorate," *American Journal of International Law,* vol. 33 (1939), pp. 714-15.

this case, or as an instrument for peaceful settlement is a healthy approach to reducing tensions in an important region of the world.[24]

Egypt and the Sudan

The Nile Valley provides an excellent example of a region that comprises a geographical unity, but its history provides ample evidence that the northern (Egypt) and the southern (Sudan) parts have not always been prepared to be united politically. After long separation since the Arab conquest, Egypt conquered the Sudan in 1821 and the two countries became part of the Ottoman Empire, although Cairo had more to say about Sudan's administration than did Constantinople. In 1899, after another separation and reconquest, Sudan became a condominium, jointly administered by Egypt and Great Britain. Their agreement of January 19, 1899 constituted the basic document relating to the juristic status of the Sudan. Article 1 defined the boundary between Egypt and the Sudan as the 22nd parallel of latitude, subject to certain qualifications. As Lord Cromer, then Britain's consul general in Egypt, explained to the British foreign secretary in presenting the draft agreement for approval:

> This article gives a definition of the territories which, for the purpose of the present convention, will be comprised in the Soudan. I should mention, by way of explanation, that the 22nd parallel of latitude runs a few miles north of Wadi Halfa. Suakin is well south of this line.
>
> If we wish to be perfectly consistent with the principles more or less explicitly set forth in the preamble, the term Soudan should be strictly limited to the territories which formerly belonged to Egypt, which were subsequently held by the Dervishes, and which, at one time or another, have been reconquered with British assistance. To do this, however, will create great administrative inconvenience for we shall then have to exclude Suakin and Wadi Halfa from the Soudan. Neither of these towns has ever been occupied by the Dervishes although it would be perfectly correct as a matter of fact to say that, but for the defensive action taken from time to time by British troops and under British auspices they would certainly have been lost to Egypt during the rebellion.
>
> It will be observed that in this article the territories comprised in the Soudan are divided into three categories. These are:
>
> (1) Those "which have never been evacuated by Egyptian troops since the year 1882." This formula has been adopted to include Wadi Halfa and Suakin.
>
> (2) Those "which, having before the late rebellion in the Soudan been administered by the Government of His Highness the Khedive, were temporarily lost to Egypt and have been reconquered by Her Majesty's Government and the Egyptian Government acting in concert." Under this heading will be included all the territory recently

---

[24] For a summary of the role of the secretary-general and his good offices in the final settlement of the Bahrain dispute, see Edward Gordon, "Resolution of the Bahrain Dispute," *American Journal of International Law,* vol. 65 (1971), pp. 560-68.

In preparing the historical portion of this section on Bahrain, the author has drawn from his article cited in footnote 5 above.

EGYPT-SUDAN NILE

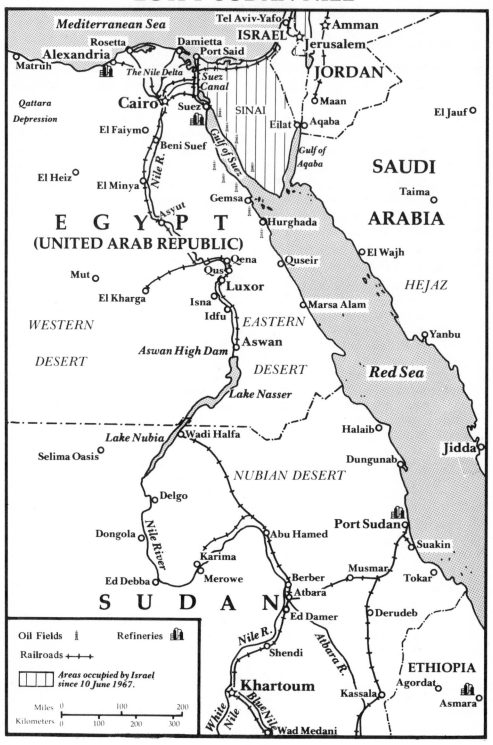

Mediterranean Sea

Rosetta Damietta
Alexandria Port Said
Matruh
The Nile Delta
Suez
Canal

ISRAEL Tel Aviv-Yafo ☆ Amman
Jerusalem
JORDAN

Cairo Suez
Qattara
Depression
El Faiym
Beni Suef
SINAI
Maan
Eilat Aqaba
El Jauf

El Heiz
El Minya
Gulf of Aqaba
Gulf of Suez
SAUDI
Taima

E G Y P T
(UNITED ARAB REPUBLIC)
Asyut
Gemsa
Hurghada
ARABIA
El Wajh

Mut
El Kharga
Qena
Qus
Luxor
Isna
Idfu
Quseir
Marsa Alam
HEJAZ
Yanbu

WESTERN
DESERT
EASTERN
Aswan
Aswan High Dam
DESERT
Lake Nasser
Red Sea

Lake Nubia Wadi Halfa
Selima Oasis
Halaib
Dungunab
Jidda

NUBIAN DESERT

Delgo
Dongola
Karima
Ed Debba Merowe
Abu Hamed
Port Sudan
Suakin
Musmar
Berber
Atbara
Tokar
Derudeb

S U D A N
Ed Damer

Nile R.
Shendi
Atbara R.
ETHIOPIA
Agordat
Khartoum Kassala
Asmara
White Nile Blue Nile
Wad Medani

Legend:
Oil Fields
Railroads
Refineries
Areas occupied by Israel
since 10 June 1967.

Miles 0   100   200
Kilometers 0   100   200   300

reconquered. There is an objection to saying "all the territory which formerly belonged to Egypt" (or words to that effect) without any limitation as to reconquest by an Anglo-Egyptian force, as the use of these words might be held to include part of the Equatorial Province, and even possibly Zeyla and Berbera, which, of course, are not intended to be included in the present agreement.

(3) Those "which may hereafter be reconquered by the two Governments acting in concert." This provision has been so worded as to include extensions southwards or westwards, acquired by Anglo-Egyptian action, and at the same time to exclude extensions from Uganda northwards, made by the English Government acting alone.[25]

Since Egypt had passed under British occupation in 1882, the government of the Sudan came under the control of Cairo, where the sirdar (commander) of the Egyptian army exercised military control of the two countries. In 1899 and 1907 the boundaries between the Sudan and Egypt were altered by administrative decrees. Some areas to the north of latitude 22° North were placed under the joint Anglo-Egyptian administration of the Sudan, and some areas to the south of latitude 22° North were placed under Egyptian administration. The areas that passed to Sudanese administration comprised the lands of the Red Sea coast north of latitude 22° and a strip astride the Nile north of Wadi Halfa. These administrative arrangements, remaining in force until the Sudan declared its independence in 1956, were considered by Sudan as constituting the final boundaries. The Provisional Constitution of the Sudan stipulated that the territory of the Sudan was to comprise "all those territories which were included in the Anglo-Egyptian Sudan immediately before the commencement of this Constitution."

On February 1, 1958, Egypt sent a note to the Sudan asserting that the Sudan had no right to include in the Sudanese electoral constituencies the area to the north of latitude 22°. It invoked the 1899 agreement and demanded the abolition of the administrative measures taken with regard to this area and a return to the political boundaries. The Egyptian government indicated its willingness to return to the Sudan the area south of the latitude 22° which was under its administration. Neither the exchange of notes nor Egyptian police could prevent the elections then being held in the disputed area, but the incident raised an interesting legal question of sovereignty over the area in question.

Direct negotiations between the Sudan and Egypt opened when the Sudanese foreign minister went to Cairo on February 18, 1958. Following the initial negotiation, a statement was issued by the Egyptian government (February 19, 1958) to the effect that Egypt proposed to the Sudan that neither party was to conduct an election campaign or a plebiscite in the disputed area until they had arrived at an amicable solution. On February 20 the Sudan requested the secretary-general of the United Nations to bring the dispute to the Security Council on the ground that Egypt had concentrated troops near the Sudan borders. Egypt requested the council to postpone action, pending direct negotiations on the

---

[25] Article 1 states: "The word 'Soudan' in this Agreement means all the territories south of the 22nd parallel of latitude. . . ." Hurewitz, *Diplomacy,* vol. I, pp. 210-18.

matter. The Security Council did not take action, although the case remained on the agenda.

The Sudan's case was based not merely on the ground that the disputed area had been transferred by Egypt's own free action, but also on the ground of the affinity of the population, inasmuch as the tribes in both the Wadi Halfa and in the Red Sea area were said to belong to the tribes residing in the area within undisputed Sudan territory. If Egypt should agree to hold a plebiscite, said the Sudanese, the differences might be settled by an expression of the wishes of the people of the disputed area.

From a strictly legal viewpoint, it can be argued that the 1899 agreement is still valid and therefore should be the instrument to define the political boundaries between Egypt and the Sudan—that is, that latitude 22°, as Article 1 indicates, forms the boundary line between the two countries. Adjustments made subsequently by Egypt for administrative purposes were of questionable validity in the absence of consent of the parties to the 1899 agreement. Short of direct negotiation, the dispute might be settled either by arbitration or adjudication. Unless it is settled, this is another pending issue that might disturb tranquillity between two neighboring Arab states, although the takeover of Sudan in 1969 by a nationalist military regime sympathetic to that of Egypt has probably reduced the likelihood of violent confrontation that existed a decade ago.

The River Jordan and Its Tributaries

The partition of Palestine, discussed in Chapter II, raised to an international level the question of utilization of the waters of the Jordan River. A portion of the Jordan became the boundary between Israel and two of the Arab states, Syria and Jordan, in accordance with the armistice agreements of 1949. Although Israel's occupation of the Golan Heights in 1967 has made the problem academic as far as Syria is concerned, at least for the time being, the Jordan River still forms part of the boundary between Israel and Jordan.

The waters of the River Jordan are limited because the rainfall in the whole region is very scant and its distribution is very uneven. The headwaters of the river rise in Syria and Israel. It becomes the boundary between Israel on the one side and Syria and Jordan on the other between Lake Hula (Huleh) and Lake Tiberias. From the north of this lake, the boundaries between Jordan and Israel move a little eastward into Jordan to include the entire Lake Tiberias to the Yarmuk tributary. Then the boundaries follow the river to a point about two-fifths of the distance from Lake Tiberias to the Dead Sea, leaving the so-called West Bank assigned to Jordan in accordance with the Jordan-Israel Armistice Agreement (though now occupied by Israel). The area on the East Bank in Jordan is known as East al-Ghawr (al-Ghor).

The River Jordan lies in a region known as the Rift—a valley splitting the mountains into two. Lake Hula, the meeting place of most of the headwaters, is just above sea level. From this point the river falls sharply to Lake Tiberias, or Sea of Galilee, about 15 miles southward, which lies 682 feet below sea level. From this lake the steep descent continues to the Dead Sea which, as the crow flies, is about 70 miles. The Dead Sea is 1,292 feet below sea level, and the Rift reaches its lowest point about the middle of the lake. From this point it begins to rise to above sea level in the southern desert and then again slopes gradually down to the Gulf of Aqaba.

Disputes over water distribution are perhaps best resolved by direct negotiation whereby the riparian states lay down their own rules of procedure. But if, as argued by Arab jurists, a state of war is still in existence between Israel and the Arab states, the armistice agreements provide rules governing the de facto situation. Since the Arab states have not accorded recognition to Israel, direct negotiation would appear to be excluded. However, the key Arab states have accepted the United Nations resolution of November 22, 1967, embodying the principles of termination of belligerency and the acceptance of fixed frontiers. In due course, in connection with negotiations to implement the resolution, they may well be prepared to discuss the dispute in accordance with the rules and principles of law. What are the rules applicable to water apportionment as they apply to the Jordan River?

Textbook writers have laid down the following general rule: Obstruction or diversion of the flow of a river by an upper riparian state to the detriment of a lower is forbidden on the principle that "no state is allowed to alter the natural conditions of its own territory to the disadvantage of the natural conditions of the territory of a neighboring state." [26] This rule is based partly on the practice of riparian states and partly on judicial precedents. Interestingly enough, the most helpful precedents are those established in the decisions of the United States Supreme Court in a number of interstate disputes over water rights. The most significant case was that between the states of Kansas and Colorado, brought to the Supreme Court in 1901. The dispute was over the Arkansas River, which flows for 280 miles through Colorado before entering Kansas. Kansas complained that a large irrigation project undertaken by Colorado would exhaust the river to such an extent that Kansas would not have enough water for its needs. The arguments presented to the Court stressed two conflicting principles of law. Kansas relied mainly on the common-law rule of riparian rights, which forbids an upper riparian owner to interfere to any extent with the flow of water which would naturally reach the owner of the lower land. Colorado invoked the principle of public ownership of flowing water (i.e., state sovereignty) and held that it was entitled to exercise its full rights with the water upon its territory. In 1907 the Supreme Court formulated its own rule of "equality of rights and equity between the two states," which forbids any interference with the flow of water "to the extent of destroying the equitable apportionment of benefits between the two states resulting from the flow of the river." [27] The principle of the "equitable apportionment of benefits" became the precedent which many textbook writers stressed as the guiding rule in similar situations. Obviously the word "equitable" did not mean "equal" in the literal sense because the equities could not be strictly quantified. In several cases

---

[26] W. E. Hall, *International Law,* ed. Pearce Higgins (Oxford, 1924), p. 175; L. Oppenheim, *International Law,* ed. H. Lauterpacht (London, 1955), vol. I, p. 474.

[27] *Kansas* v. *Colorado* et al., 206 U.S. (1907). See also Green H. Hackworth, *Digest of International Law* (Washington, 1940), vol. I, pp. 580-81.

such as *Wyoming* v. *Colorado* (1922), *Connecticut* v. *Massachusetts* (1930) and others the rule of equitable apportionment was applied, and this rule seems to be gaining general acceptance.[28]

The American practice has influenced European actions and legal decisions. Since World War II there has been a tendency to reformulate general rules applicable to the question of the diversion of international rivers and the apportionment of their waters, based on technical proposals of experts. In its meetings of 1956 and 1958 the International Law Association adopted the generally accepted practices of states as guiding principles, stressing the right of each riparian state to a "reasonable" and "equitable" use of the water, provided no "injury" is done to another state. In the practice of states, there has also been the tendency to seek the advice of international supervisory commissions for either individual or joint utilization of water resources.[29]

Several attempts have been made to apportion the waters of the Jordan River either on the basis of the principle of equitable apportionment or on proposals made by a third party. Some embodied ambitious schemes of economic development for the mutual benefit of riparian states. The first such proposals were made as early as the Mandate period, before Israel was established, and there have been various others since that time.[30] Perhaps the most constructive approach was the attempt by the United States in 1952 to work out a plan which would benefit all riparian states and also alleviate the refugee problem. President Eisenhower appointed Eric Johnston, a former president of the United States Chamber of Commerce, to negotiate with the states involved a newly prepared plan, called the Main Plan, to be implemented partly by United Nations technical assistance and partly with the aid of private business. It was prepared at the request of the United Nations Relief and Works Agency for Palestine Refugees (UNRWA) by the Tennessee Valley Authority (TVA), based on past proposals for the utilization of the Jordan River. The proposals, formally entitled *The Unified Development of the Water Resources of the Jordan Valley Region,* became the basis for the negotiations conducted by Johnston during 1953-55. It was understood that the unified development of the Jordan system would be financed largely by United States funds.

The Main Plan attempted to reconcile, on the basis of practicality and economy, proposals made specifically for the benefit of Israel or Jordan, because each

---

[28] See James Simsarian, "The Diversion of Waters Affecting The United States and Canada," *American Journal of International Law,* vol. 32 (1938), pp. 488-518.

[29] See H. A. Smith, *The Economic Use of International Rivers* (London, 1931); W. E. Kenworthy, "Joint Development of International Waters," *American Journal of International Law,* vol. 54 (1960), pp. 596-602; O. Z. Ghobashi, *The Development of the Jordan River* (New York, 1961), pp. 36-41.

[30] In 1943 the Jewish Agency sought the advice of Walter C. Lowdermilk, Assistant Chief of the Soil Conservation Service of the United States, whose survey was published in a book entitled, *Palestine, Land of Promise* (Washington, 1946). He proposed that the waters of the upper Jordan be diverted primarily to satisfy the Jewish population. This was followed by a series of other studies, especially after the creation of Israel, by J. B. Hays, A. L. Savage, and others. Jordan also sought expert advice and a number of surveys were made for the utilization of the Yarmuk River. These plans were later studied and reconciled by the Johnston Mission. For a brief account of these plans, see M. G. Ionides, "The Disputed Waters of Jordan," *Middle East Journal,* vol. VII (1953), pp. 153-64; Ghobashi, *Development of Jordan River,* pp. 12-21.

110

would divert a disproportionate quantity of the water at the expense of the other. As Mrs. Stevens has summed it up:

> The study started with the premise that the Jordan waters must be utilized within the Jordan River watershed. This was to be accomplished by storage on the Hasbani River in Lebanon and a power drop to the floor of the Jordan Valley. A canal would then carry Jordan headwaters by gravity along the western, Israeli side of the upper Jordan Valley. On the eastern side of the valley the plan proposed irrigation of the Yarmuk plateau region, and a power station and dam at Adasiya, with a canal from this point to Lake Tiberias. Water from Tiberias would be channeled down both sides of the Jordan to the lower Jordan Valley.[31]

It took two years for Eric Johnston to persuade Israel and negotiating subcabinet officials of the Arab states to accept a modified plan which would provide 40 percent of the Jordan water to Israel and 60 percent for Lebanon, Syria, and Jordan without any restrictions for irrigation plans within any one of these states. The political atmosphere was most unfavorable, and the plan was finally rejected by the Arab governments mainly because it was construed to imply recognition of Israel and settlement of the refugee problem without Israel's acceptance of the principles of repatriation or compensation. Nor was Israel satisfied with Johnston's plan because it meant restrictions on its designs to divert more water for the development of the desert area in the Negev.[32]

The failure of a plan put forward by a third party for direct or indirect United Nations assistance meant that each of the riparian states would carry out its own plan for water utilization independently, with consequential encroachments on each other's rights. Israel, in greater need of water than her Arab neighbors, began to implement ambitious plans to provide for an increasing population as well as for the irrigation of her southern desert territory.

In 1964 a plan known as the National Water Carrier—a 70-mile series of canals, tunnels, and giant pipelines extending from a point on the northwestern shore of Lake Tiberias down to a point southeast of Tel Aviv—was launched to connect an already completed system, known as the Yarkon-Negev pipeline, thus bringing Jordan waters to the heart of the desert lands of the Negev. At the start, the conduit was to carry 150 to 180 million cubic meters annually. When it was completed, it was expected to draw some 320 million cubic meters (about 84 billion gallons) of the Jordan waters annually.

The Arab states, considering the Israeli plan an encroachment on their riparian rights, discussed at a summit meeting in Cairo early in 1964 schemes which would counteract the Israeli project. They considered diverting the two chief sources of the River Jordan—the Hasbani in Lebanon and the Banyas in Syria—in order to prevent their flow into Israel. Detailed plans of construction were discussed later in the year and funds to finance the project were sought from domestic and foreign sources. The Soviet Union and China offered to contribute. Plans were completed and several Arab states were designated to provide funds, but innumerable

---

[31] Georgiana Q. Stevens, "The Jordan River Valley," *International Conciliation* (January 1956), pp. 261-62.

[32] Ibid., p. 263; Don Peretz, "Development of the Jordan Valley Waters," *Middle East Journal,* vol. IX (1955), pp. 397-412.

obstacles, political as well as technical, frustrated the program. Only Jordan completed the East Ghor Canal, begun in 1958, which drew water from the Yarmuk River and irrigated an area for some 50 miles south of that river.[33] This canal system was directly in the line of fire during the June war of 1967, and has been repeatedly damaged during the recurrent outbreaks of hostilities since that time.

Allocation of the Nile Waters

After a short visit to Egypt in ancient times, Herodotus remarked that Egypt was the gift of the Nile. This remark is not only still true for Egypt, but also for the Sudan, because the Nile is the only important source of water for these two countries and for certain areas of Ethiopia as well. When the Sudan was in a condominium status (see earlier section), the Nile was under the control of a single authority in Cairo. It was during the Anglo-Egyptian administration that perennial irrigation was introduced. Arrangements for the allocation of the Nile waters were made on the basis of surveys undertaken by British engineers. Since Egypt is virtually rainless and a relatively overpopulated agricultural country, Great Britain took these factors into consideration in the allocation of the Nile waters. Britain signed agreements with Italy and Ethiopia so that sufficient waters would be allowed to flow into the Sudan without interference if dams were constructed upstream.

Britain's principal concern was to provide a scheme that would allow Egypt to use sufficient amounts of water without adversely affecting Sudanese agricultural development. Plans for the construction of dams were laid down to enable Egypt to store water during flood periods for use when the Nile waters became low. Preparation for the implementation of such plans took a very long time, due to differences between Egypt and Britain, the controlling authorities over the Sudan, on water allocation and other technical matters.

In 1929 an agreement was finally reached in which Egypt's utilization of the Nile waters in accordance with her needs (as defined in technical reports) was recognized, but it was realized that the development of the Sudan required a quantity of the Nile waters greater than that hitherto utilized. An increase in the quantity of waters for the Sudan's needs was agreed upon provided it did not infringe Egypt's "natural and historical rights in the waters of the Nile and its requirements of agricultural extension." [34]

This agreement, becoming the basis of all subsequent arrangements of water allocation, has been viewed differently by various writers. Egyptian writers held that the agreement has merely recorded Egypt's established rights over the Nile basin since antiquity.[35] To others, the agreement provided an international regime for the Nile basin as a whole in which several countries were involved, although the paramountcy of Egypt's agricultural interests were recognized.[36]

[33] See J. L. Dees, "Jordan's East Ghor Canal Project," *Middle East Journal,* vol. XIII (1959), pp. 357-70.

[34] For full text of the agreement, see *Notes in Regard to the Use of the Waters of the Nile* (London: His Majesty's Stationery Office, 1929), Cmd. 3348.

[35] S. al-Manqabadi, *Tatawwur al-Markaz al-Dawli li al-Sudan* (Cairo, 1958), p. 324.

[36] C. A. Pompe, "The Nile Waters Questions," *Symbolae Verzijl* (1958), p. 281.

MIDDLE EAST AND THE NILE

EUROPE

Black Sea

Caspian

U.S.S.R.

Aral Sea

Turkish Straits

Euphrates Basin

Baku

GREECE

Ankara

TURKEY

Sea

A S I A

Teheran

CYPRUS

SYRIA

IRAQ

IRAN

AFGHANISTAN

Mediterranean Sea

LEBANON

Jordan Valley

Damascus

Baghdad

ISRAEL

Amman

Benghazi

Suez Canal

Jerusalem

KUWAIT

Shatt al-Arab

JORDAN

Kuwait

PAKISTAN

Cairo

Suez Canal & Aqaba

Najd

BAHRAIN

LIBYA

EGYPT

Hejaz

SAUDI

QATAR

(U.A.R.)

TRUCIAL STATES

Muscat

Aswan High Dam

Red

Riyadh

ARABIA

Mecca

Bahrain & Persian Gulf States

CHAD

Sea

MUSCAT & OMAN

Nile R.

Hadhramaut

SOUTHERN

YEMEN

Egypt-Sudan Nile

Khartoum

YEMEN

Sana

SUDAN

Blue Nile

Djibouti

Aden

A F R I C A

Bab el Mandeb

CENTRAL
AFRICAN REP.

White Nile

Addis Ababa

ETHIOPIA

SOMALIA

Indian Ocean

Mogadishu

UGANDA

KENYA

CONGO

RWANDA

L. Victoria

Sources of the Nile

BURUNDI

TANZANIA

Miles 0   500   1000

Kilometers 0   500   1000   1500

Areas outline separately designed maps.

113

Before this agreement was concluded, Egypt acted as if the Nile were her national property.

Although certain subsequent modifications have been made, especially since 1952, giving the Sudan certain rights to store more water in one of its reservoirs, the 1929 agreement remained the basic instrument regulating water allocation.

Egypt's need for further irrigation prompted her experts to lay down a plan for a water reservoir through construction of the High Dam at Aswan (recently completed with Soviet assistance). This plan became one of the fundamental reconstruction schemes of the Egyptian revolutionary regime. Since this project, designed to create the second largest artificial lake in the world (a length of over 500 km, a width of an average of 12 km, and a maximum depth of 97 meters), would require a considerable quantity of water, the question of the utilization of the Nile water became again the subject of debate between Egypt and the Sudan. After protracted negotiations, a new agreement was concluded in 1959, based on the 1929 agreement and taking into consideration changes in population and irrigation plans of the two countries.

The 1959 agreement is more comprehensive than previous ones, in that it embodies a scheme for the complete control of the Nile waters as well as complete machinery for the regulation of works needed for the exploitation of the Nile at present and in the future for the mutual interests of the two riparian states. The agreement may be summarized as follows:

First, while it reaffirmed the principles embodied in the 1929 agreement, it also laid down rules for future agricultural development.

Second, the agreement redefined the principle of established rights that had been accepted in previous agreements by allocating to the Sudan a greater proportion of water than before, based on the actual use of water at the time the agreement was concluded. This proportion of allocation is taken to constitute the established rights of the two riparian states. The two parties, however, agreed to review the amounts of water used by each other and to check whether each had actually utilized the water it had derived. They also were to check whether utilization by one imposed hardship or injury on the other, taking into consideration that each party ensures that what was utilized was the true and just expression of its need. At least to these two Nile riparian states, the principle of established rights had been accepted. It may well become a precedent for other riparian states to adopt as a rule of international law.

Third, the new arrangement raised the Sudan's share of Nile waters from 1/12 of Egypt's share under the 1929 agreement to 1/3 of Egypt's under the new agreement. This went a long way to meet the Sudan's demand for an equitable apportionment of the Nile waters. The other party's share is determined not only on the basis of established rights but also on other considerations such as need. If the average natural flow of the Nile proved to be more than estimated, the two parties would equally share in the increase. If the claims of other riparian states proved to be consistent with their needs, they should be deducted equally from the share of the two parties.

Fourth, the rights of construction of control works, whether undertaken by the United Arab Republic or the Sudan, were specifically defined in the new agreement. For instance, the construction of the Aswan High Dam and the Roseris Reservoir were specifically mentioned to be approved by the two parties.[37] While the agreement permitted each party to undertake control works subject to prior approval of the other, it made it clear that such rights should not be exercised to an extent that would interfere with the natural flow of the Nile, save with the consent of the other party.

Fifth, if any injuries resulted from the control works undertaken by one party to the other, responsibility for the damage would be accepted by the party causing the injury and compensation would be paid to the other. The principle of compensation for damage done by one riparian state to another has been accepted by other states as binding on riparian states.

Finally, the agreement created a permanent Joint Technical Committee with powers to draw up unified development plans, to collect data and direct research, to supervise the execution of development plans, to draw up working arrangements and operating control works, to study and recommend measures in the event of an impending shortage of water supply, and to study and recommend a unified water policy for the two parties vis-à-vis other riparian states.[38]

This agreement, putting an end to a long standing controversy over the allocation of the Nile waters, may well be regarded as the example *par excellence* for settlement of disputes between two Middle Eastern countries by peaceful methods. It is a case which may well set a precedent for other disputes to be settled by peaceful methods, if the parties were willing to subordinate narrow local to regional interests.[39]

The Euphrates River

In the last 20 years, taking advantage of increased technological and financial resources, the three riparians of the Euphrates River basin, Turkey, Syria, and Iraq, have developed and started to implement ambitious plans to exploit the waters of the Euphrates which, along with the Tigris, has meant the difference between life and death to the people of Mesopotamia since the Garden of Eden. If all their plans are carried out, the demand for water will exceed the available supply. This increased interest has been accompanied by an increase in "river politics" and a concurrent though intermittent movement toward negotiations among the riparians aimed at an equitable sharing of the river's water supply. In this process, each state has enunciated its interests in the basin and has developed a legal and negotiating position to promote those interests. While evolving principles of international law must eventually be brought to bear on the problem,

---

[37] Article 2(1) states: The two Republics agree to the construction by the U.A.R. of the Sudd al-Ali Reservoir at Aswan as the first of a series of overyear storage schemes on the Nile.

Article 2(2) states: The two Republics agree to the construction by the Sudan Republic of the Roseris Reservoir on the Blue Nile and any other works deemed necessary by the Sudan.

[38] For full text of the 1959 agreement, see *Revue Egyptien de Droit International,* vol. 15 (1959), pp. 321-25.

[39] For studies on these questions, see G. M. Badr, "The Nile Waters Question," *Revue Egyptien de Droit International,* vol. 15 (1959), pp. 94-117; Syed Hosni, "The Nile Regime," ibid., vol. 17 (1961), pp. 70-99; and Abd al-Fattah I. S. Baddour, *Sudanese-Egyptian Relations* (The Hague, 1960), pp. 201-41.

EUPHRATES BASIN

unilateral statements concerning water usage have occupied more attention than legal formulations in recent years.

The Euphrates basin includes some 350,000 square kilometers, of which 110,-000 are in eastern Turkey, 70,000 in Syria, and 170,000 in Iraq.[40] As the river approaches the delta and the Persian Gulf, the land beside the river becomes increasingly barren. The headwaters in Turkey contribute the largest portion of the water supply of the river.[41] There are a few tributaries in Syria which account for the fertility of the Jazira province, but these add little, compared to tributaries in Turkey, to the basin of the Euphrates. Any systematic use of the waters would

---

[40] See especially R. Hartman and Etienne de Vaumas, "al-Furat," *The Encyclopedia of Islam, New Edition,* vol. III (Leiden: Brill), pp. 945-48.

[41] Wafiq Husain al-Khashab, *The Water Budget of the Tigris and Euphrates Basin* (Chicago: University of Chicago, Department of Geography, 1958) pp. 38-39.

depend on many factors, such as settlement patterns, national wealth, and rainfall. Prior to 1960, only Iraq made systematic use of the river's waters: pressing irrigation needs and flood control problems demanded such attention. Several studies were made, in particular those by Sir William Willrock, Lord Salter, and Alexander Gibb & Company; projects included the development of the depressions at Bahr al-Milh and Habbaniya.[42] Recently, Iraq has been able to control the river completely from the town of Hit. Several canals, including a big one at Ramadi, have aided Iraq's irrigation and flood control efforts.

Since the 1950s, both Syria and Turkey have started to make clear their own interests in the basin. Their comparative lack of interest in the river prior to the 1950s was due primarily to the greater concern for and financial commitment to other projects: for Syria, agricultural development in the West, in particular the Ghab project on the Orontes River; and for Turkey, the expansion of hydroelectric power and irrigation in the western and central regions. Where private enterprise once developed irrigation projects, the Syrian government moved in and developed the Khabur River of the Jazira province and at the same time drafted plans for a huge dam on the Euphrates.[43] The government was interested in the development of the Euphrates basin because it had the capacity of creating jobs in the area of Syria's chief export—agricultural produce—and of alleviating population pressures in Western Syria. For this large plan, Syria was willing to solicit foreign help. At first the West Germans were interested. After certain political disagreements, the Syrians turned to the Soviet Union. Through Soviet-Syrian agreements in April and May of 1966, plans for the first stage of the Tabaqa Dam were issued, and work commenced in 1969. The first stage, originally scheduled for completion in 1972, would irrigate some 200,000 hectares. Progress has reportedly been slower than expected, partly because of various Soviet apprehensions, including the lack of any agreement among the riparians on water rights. If this dam were completed, it would naturally produce significant repercussions in Iraq.

Turkey is also developing and trying to implement plans for exploiting the Euphrates waters. The five-year plan of 1963-67 called for use of the headwaters to meet electrical power demands for new industries located in eastern Anatolia, still the least developed part of Turkey.[44] The hydroelectric project at Keban was begun in 1963. It was not to consume water, but merely change the seasonal flow by eliminating the extreme fluctuations of flow that formerly threatened the property and livelihood of the persons living farther down the river in Syria and Iraq.

---

[42] Sir William Willcocks, *Irrigation of Mesopotamia,* 2nd ed. (London: Spon, 1917); James Salter, *The Development of Iraq* (n.p.: Iraq Development Board, 1955); Government of Syria, *Taqrir al-Sir Alixandar Jibb wa Shuraka'ih,* 1947 (Damascus: Matarat al-Jumhuriyya al-Suriyya, 1950, in Arabic).

[43] Uthman al-A'idi, "Mashru Sadd al-Furat" in *Government of Syria,* al-Majlis al-A'la Li al-Ulum, *Mahrajan Usbu al-Ilm al-Thalith* (Damascus: April 1962), vol. I, pp. 30-54 (in Arabic).

[44] Turkey, State Planning Organization, *First Five Year Development Plan, 1963-1967* (Ankara: 1963), pp. 356-58.

International Law and the Euphrates. Legal doctrine relating to riparian rights has already been touched on briefly in connection with the Nile waters, above. The Euphrates is more complicated because three states are involved, and they do not always see eye to eye. International legal theorists have, at various times, enunciated four principles as possible foundations for a system of water law governing the exploitation of water flowing through more than one state.[45] These are as follows: (1) the principle of absolute territorial sovereignty, which would allow a state to use as it wishes waters flowing through its territory, but would not allow a state to demand the continued free flow of such water from other riparians; (2) the principle of absolute territorial integrity, which would give a state the right to demand the continuation of the natural flow of water coming from other countries, but not the right to restrict the natural flow of waters proceeding through its territory into other countries; (3) the principle of "community in the waters," which would vest rights in the collective body of riparians, permitting the waters to be divided proportionately, or allowing the creation of some other kind of regime whereby no one state could exploit the waters without the positive cooperation of the other riparians; and (4) a principle restricting the free use of the waters which, while not extending as far as the principle of community in the waters, restricts in varying degrees the principle of absolute territorial sovereignty just as it does that of absolute territorial integrity.

Much emphasis has been placed on the fourth principle. The International Law Association at its September 1958 meeting in New York, expressing the law as it exists, enumerated the following principles:

> 1. A system of rivers and lakes in drainage basins should be treated as an integrated whole.
>
> 2. Except as otherwise provided by treaty or other instruments or customs binding upon the parties, each co-riparian state is entitled to a reasonable and equitable share of the beneficial uses of the waters of the drainage basin. What amounts to a reasonable and equitable share is a question to be determined in the light of all the relevant factors in each particular case.
>
> 3. Co-riparian states are under a duty to respect the legal rights of each co-riparian state in the drainage basin.[46]

The proposed Syrian dam on the Euphrates does not appear to protect adequately the rights of other riparians. But this criticism can be directed at the other co-riparians as well: it reflects the lack of international treaties and conventions on regulation of the Euphrates. Perhaps this is not surprising in view of the fact that two of the states involved (Iraq and Syria) only recently became independent. To date there has been only one convention of substance: the Turko-Iraqi "Treaty of Friendship and Neighborly Relations," which came into force in 1948. The first protocol annexed to this treaty states that Turkey and Iraq:

> . . . recognizing the importance . . . for Iraq . . . of the construction of conservation works on the Tigris and Euphrates and their tributaries,

---

[45] Friedrich J. Berber, *Rivers in International Law* (London: Stevens, 1959), pp. 13-14.
[46] Ibid., pp. 42-44.

in order to ensure the maintenance of a regular water supply and the regulation of the water flow of the two rivers with a view to avoiding the danger of floods during the annual periods of high-water, . . . considering that it will probably be found after investigation that the most suitable sites for the construction of dams and other similar works, the entire cost of which shall be defrayed by Iraq, lie in Turkish territory, being also in agreement upon the installation of permanent observation stations in Turkish territory to record the water flow of the above-mentioned rivers and to communicate regularly to Iraq the results of these observations, . . . accepting in principle that any of the conservation works which may be built upon these waters should be adapted, as far as is possible, to the interests of both countries for the purposes of irrigation and the production of hydroelectric power . . . have agreed as follows: [47]

The protocol goes on to provide other forms of cooperation between Iraq and Turkey.[48]

So far, however, international conventions on the Euphrates and general international legal principles have contributed little to any solution of the legal and political problems involving Iraq, Syria, and Turkey in the Euphrates basin: relevant conventions are few in number and international legal norms have been slow in evolving. Hence the question remains: to what degree are the riparians, by agreement, willing to limit their own free use of their waters?

River Cooperation and Negotiations. Cooperation among the three riparians on the Euphrates has so far been limited to information exchanges and joint studies. The establishment of a "Euphrates River Authority" or some such intergovernmental organization empowered to allocate the waters is invoked from time to time, but the possibilities of such action seem remote at present. During the 1950s Turkish and Iraqi politicians and water experts discussed many water problems together, sometimes within the context of the Baghdad Pact. A remnant of this exchange can still be seen, but it is complicated by a completely different political atmosphere since the Iraqi Revolution of July 14, 1958. Turko-Syrian cooperation has never been notable on any subject, and Syrian-Iraqi cooperation has been limited in recent years by the vagaries of inter-Arab politics involving competing factions of the Baath party.

Examination of the water interests of the three parties indicates that there may be definite possibilities for cooperation for mutual economic benefit. Iraq's major interest is in maintaining the flow of water so that it can irrigate the rich lands of the lower Euphrates valley. A water conservation agreement with Turkey and Syria and an agreement with Syria over the flow of water from the proposed Tabaqa dam would definitely be in Iraq's interests. Likewise, Syria has an interest in a conservation agreement, an allocation agreement maximizing the potential of the Tabaqa complex, and an agreement with Turkey over the amount of water to be released by the Keban Dam. Syria's bargaining position, moreover, is strong, especially since its river-development designs are still in the pre-investment stage.

---

[47] See United Nations, *Treaty Series XXXVII* (1949), pp. 256-87.
[48] Ibid., pp. 251, 287-91.

Syria has the option of bargaining away some of her estimated capacity for other concessions, perhaps of a political nature. Turkey's main concern seems to be a water allocation agreement which would permit her, at some future time, to expand irrigation projects to the area below the Keban Dam.

The official position of Iraq, the status quo power of the basin, has been consistent for many years. Iraq stresses its water rights acquired over the years and demands that the other riparians respect those rights: Syria, whose ambitious plans threaten the status quo, is thus the target of many Iraqi admonitions. Brigadier Abd al-Karim Qasim, the Iraqi head of state, issued this warning on September 23, 1961:

> In Syria they can dispose only of the quantity of water which they were using before without affecting others' shares. They can not dispose of a quantity of water more than the limited share and if they do so, they will then be in a critical position from the international aspect. . . . The Euphrates is in our country and those who want to build a dam, they have to come to make an understanding with us. No one can march on the wrong side.[49]

An Iraqi water expert stated this position in more delicate terms:

> The rights and obligations of any riparian state concerning the case of the waters of international rivers like the Euphrates are fairly well defined and governed by the provisions of international law which, by the way, places a very strong emphasis on the sacredness of the acquired rights regarding the water required for the already established projects and services. In this respect and to that extent, Iraq's acquired water rights are fairly well covered by the terms of international law . . . it is imperative that the riparian states must first agree on defining their respective shares out of the balance between acquired rights and the annual discharge of the river. . . .[50]

The Syrian position appears to be less consistent and somewhat more innovative. While Syria does use precepts of international law to develop its case, it fluctuates between claiming absolute control over the Euphrates waters in its territory and calling for some restricted "community in the waters." The Syrians have never, however, accepted the Iraqi position that Iraq's acquired rights are nonnegotiable. Syria considers existing patterns of water use to be inequitable, and it seeks improvements. It is particularly annoyed at the Alexander Gibb & Company study on the Euphrates, which it considers biased in Iraq's favor for political reasons. A Syrian government engineer concluded in 1962, rather moderately under the circumstances, that Iraq's "internationally recognized share" was well under one-half, while Syria's was well over one-quarter. This allocation, of course, would leave Turkey with very little, inasmuch as Turkey controls all the headwaters of the river.

Turkey appears to be more flexible than the others. While accepting the need for some restricted "community of waters," it has never defined what it considers to be its share. Turkey seems to feel no need for immediate negotiations. Regional

---

49 *The Iraq Times* (September 25, 1961), p. 1.
50 Ibid. (August 17, 1961), pp. 1, 13.

politics apparently are of greater concern to her than water needs. **Turkey's** attitude will presumably crystallize when its development requires exploitation of Euphrates waters for irrigation purposes.

Before the June war of 1967 numerous bilateral negotiations were held. The Soviet Union, anxious to start the Tabaqa complex in Syria, was reluctant to do so until the Syrians and the Iraqis reached an agreement. However, the many Syrian-Iraqi negotiations brought no Iraqi political concessions to Syria and no Syrian recognition of Iraq's acquired rights in the basin. At the same time it was negotiating with Syria, Iraq was holding similar discussions with Turkey. Indeed the exchange of Iraqi support for Turkey on Cyprus for Turkish support of Iraq on the Kurdish and Euphrates problems probably pleased the Baghdad government. The Palestine and Alexandretta issues continue to plague all Turko-Syrian relations. These relations have been the weakest link in the chain of Euphrates River development. In the end, Syria may well relinquish some of her claims in the basin in favor of Iraq: Syria can best afford to give up some of her claims—claims for the future for which finances have not yet been allocated. Syria's political and economic isolation on this issue may well lead to moderation in due course.

The Cyprus Problem

The Cyprus problem is an ethno-religious communal conflict with international dimensions. Cyprus, because of its location and size,[51] is of considerable strategic importance for Mediterranean powers, particularly the United States, the Soviet Union, Greece, and Turkey. The conflict on the island between the Greek and Turkish communities arouses emotions in both Greece and Turkey, consequently involving the governments of those countries in the politics of Cyprus.

The ideological climate of communal strife in Cyprus, which is in part the legacy of such historical forces as Pan-Hellenism, Orthodox Christianity, and Ottoman Islam, was altered and given new impetus by the introduction of the *millet* system and modern nationalism. The emotional predisposition of both the Greek and Turkish masses has been overridden, however, despite the influence of such developments, by political interests and pressures at the governmental level which make it extremely unlikely that such popular schemes as *enosis* (union) and *taksim* (partition) will be seriously pursued as practical goals. One might conclude that, although exclusive and extreme political attitudes are deeply rooted in the Greek and Turkish psyche, conciliatory and reasonable departures on the part of Greek, Turkish, and Cypriot leaders are stronger than is at first apparent. That is, the risk of seeming less patriotic than the mass demands and the possibility of resultant political suicide has not been so overpowering for Greek and Turkish political leaders as one might think.

Historically, Cyprus has had close connections with Constantinople-Istanbul, which still have an influence on the problems agitating her population and the peoples of Greece and Turkey. Most of the elements making up the Greek

---

[51] Cyprus is about 40 miles from Turkey, is about 3,600 square miles in size, and can threaten land positions in southwest Asia, including those in the Soviet Union.

Cypriot "nationality" of today, including religion and political outlook, are rooted in the era of the Greek-Byzantine empire. The period of Ottoman control saw the introduction of the Turkish minority and the establishment of the *millet* system, whereby the Greek and Turkish communities were socially and politically separated, each holding fast to its own language and religion. Another significant feature of the *millet* arrangement was the elevation of the Greek Orthodox clergy to a position of temporal power. The leadership of the Orthodox church was made responsible for the collection of taxes and was given the function of liaison with the Ottoman government.

In 1878, the British occupied Cyprus in order to check Russian expansion into the Ottoman Empire and Persia and to protect British routes through the Red Sea and the Fertile Crescent to India. Although they did not alter the basic features of Cypriot communal structure, the British did introduce measures that influenced the island's development. For example, British encouragement of business and trade benefited the Greek community more than the Turkish population. The relative political freedom allowed by the British administration, plus a liberal educational policy that left the instruction of Greek Cypriot children largely to mainland Greek nationalists, contributed to the growth of *enosist* sentiment. In the Legislative Council founded in 1881 and not abolished until 1931, the membership was constituted so that the British appointed members and the Turkish elected members together made up a majority, which often prevailed over the Greek Cypriot minority. This institutional arrangement hardened community divisions and resentments. On the other hand, British rule was in many respects beneficial to the island, particularly in the field of economic development.

After World War I, by the Treaty of Lausanne, Greece and Turkey recognized British sovereignty over Cyprus. The island was declared a Crown Colony in 1925. In the 1950s, three developments led to the independence of Cyprus. First was the overall reduction in Britain's role as an international power. Second, in the 1950s Greece and the Greek Cypriots began to use the United Nations and the principle of self-determination to advance the cause of *enosis,* and alternately of Cypriot independence. Third, in 1955 a campaign of sabotage and terrorism was launched by General Grivas and his organization EOKA to support the efforts of Archbishop Makarios and other Greek Cypriot leaders to attain either union with Greece or independence. In response, the British government gradually moved from a position of "no change of sovereignty" to acquiescence in eventual freedom of choice for both communities regarding *enosis* or partition and finally to agreement with respect to transfer of sovereignty on condition that military bases remained under British control.

February 1959 saw the construction of a legal regime to contain and structure the various forces in Cyprus. Three interdependent documents, the Treaty of Guarantee, the Treaty of Alliance, and the Basic Structure of the Republic of Cyprus, established the structure agreed upon by Great Britain, Greece, and Turkey and accepted by both Cypriot communities' leadership. The Basic Structure of the Republic set forth the principal articles of the Constitution of Cyprus upon its achieving independence in August 1960. The constitution was largely concerned with the protection of the Turkish minority, which made up about 20 percent of the total population. Modification of tax laws, electoral laws, and laws regarding municipalities required separate majorities of both the Greek and Turkish representatives in the House of Representatives. Separate Turkish municipalities were to be established in each of the five largest towns, and Turkish as well as Greek Communal Chambers were set up to enact laws relating to matters of personal status and religion. In addition, quotas were established according to which the Turkish community was guaranteed more than proportional representation in the nation's public service. Turkish Cypriot control over communal matters and an effective Turkish veto regarding vital national concerns clashed with Greek leaders' aims to expand the power of the majority and strengthen the internal structure of the state. The 1959-60 agreements ended the conflict between Great Britain and the Greek Cypriots, and they outlawed the extreme and conflicting Greek Cypriot and Turkish Cypriot goals of union with Greece and partition of the island. But those arrangements did not settle the problem of communal conflict, which still requires reconciliation of the prerogative of majority rule with the protection of minority rights.

The Constitution was agreed upon as a result of negotiations among Great Britain, Greece and Turkey, but it was resented by the Greek Cypriot majority and its leadership. Despite the obligation of Cyprus, Great Britain, Greece and Turkey to "ensure respect for the Constitution," the ironical fact was that the state of affairs created by this document appeared unacceptable to the majority of the population (or its leadership). Encroachment by the leaders of the Greek majority upon the guaranteed rights of the Turkish minority was clearly unconstitutional, but it was justified by the leadership as an assertion of independence, of sovereign right, and by virtue of *raison d'état*.

In January 1962, President Makarios declared that since the Constitution conferred rights on the Turkish Cypriots in addition to what was intended only to protect them, and since these rights were being used to obstruct the functioning of the machinery of state, he was forced to disregard or seek revision of provisions which, if abused, could endanger the state. He gave this statement of principle practical significance in December 1963 when he proposed repeal of the vice president's veto power,[52] the removal of the requirement for separate majorities in the House for vital tax and electoral legislation, and removal of the constitutional provisions for separate municipalities and the Turkish public service quotas.

Fighting erupted shortly after this announcement. Since the December 1963 crisis, the 1960 constitutional prerogatives of the Turkish community have been eroded, and few Turkish officials have remained in government posts. In the summer of 1965, the special representative of the secretary-general of the United Nations was informed that the Cyprus government no longer recognized the leader of the Turkish community in his capacity as vice president and that the Turkish Cypriot members no longer had legal standing in the House of Representatives.[53] In addition, the requirement for separate majorities in the House for

---

[52] According to the Constitution, the President of Cyprus was to be Greek, the Vice President Turkish.

[53] Secretary-general's *Report on Recent Developments in Cyprus,* U.N. Document S/6569 (1965), p. 3.

important legislation was changed. Thus by 1965 the Turks had been largely excluded from the government. New machinery was mobilized to establish a unitary state based on majority rule despite the fact that Cyprus was intended to be a state with firmly guaranteed privileges for its two separate national communities. The Cypriot government maintained that its constitution and the treaty obligations to uphold it were, in important respects, invalid since they had been forced upon her as restraints on her exercise of sovereign rights of constitutional and poliitical development. The government was in the anomalous position of subverting, in effect, its own constitution.

The contention that the 1960 agreements were invalid because they had not been arrived at in conditions allowing all parties complete freedom of choice appears specious. States cannot always deal with each other from equal bargaining positions; international agreements are frequently reached under circumstances of inequality of the parties' power and position. This does not mean that such agreements are necessarily invalid or unenforceable in international law. Denunciation of treaties on the grounds that the parties were not of equal status during the negotiation process would, if accepted as a legitimate prerogative of sovereignty, run totally counter to the well-established principle of *pacta sunt servanda*. When the leaders of both the Greek and Turkish communities declared their acceptance of the 1960 agreements, they abandoned whatever legal ground they might have had for objecting to the international negotiations that led to the conclusion of those agreements. Makarios' subsequent denunciation of the treaties and of the Cypriot Constitution was therefore of highly questionable legality, leaving aside the ethical aspects of his actions.

From the political and administrative standpoint, some revision of the 1960 Accords to provide a more coherent and cohesive governmental structure and fundamental law may have been in order. The appropriate route to change, however, was through negotiation rather than through unilateral denunciation of treaty obligations whose most important feature was protection of the Turkish minority. The treaty structure could have served as a point of departure, since it was an attempt to balance various international and national interests. The out-of-hand rejection by the Greek Cypriot leadership of the 1960 agreements illustrated precisely the Turkish Cypriot community's need for protection intended to be afforded by those very agreements.

Even more serious from the international standpoint, the Cypriot government's refusal to implement various provisions of the constitution and its breach of its treaty obligations to uphold the constitution nearly provoked Turkish armed intervention in 1964 and again in 1967. Under Article 4 of the Treaty of Guarantee, each of the guaranteeing powers (Great Britain, Greece, and Turkey) reserved the right to act to reestablish the state of affairs set up by the February 1959 Basic Structure, Treaty of Guarantee, and Treaty of Alliance. Given the violent circumstances of early 1964 and the apparent failure of concerted efforts to move the situation back to the *status quo ante* December 1963, Turkey had plausible legal grounds under the Treaty of Guarantee for intervening to protect the Turkish Cypriot population against revision by force of Cyprus' internationally guaranteed political and legal structure.

The United Nations Charter requires members to refrain from the use or threat of force against any state's territorial integrity or independence. But the rationale for Turkish action would have been maintenance and restoration of the 1960 agreements, which themselves were designed to insure the independence, territorial integrity, and security of Cyprus. The obligations of United Nations members to uphold the purposes of the Charter do not preclude the use of force in circumstances where peaceful redress of legitimate grievances is impossible. In such a situation, the use of force may be justified under international law, particularly if intended to oppose another state's illegal resort to force.

On the other hand, once the United Nations Security Council was seized of the Cyprus situation, Turkey's right to act unilaterally under the 1960 Treaty of Guarantee was materially compromised. A Security Council Resolution of March 4, 1964, called upon members to "refrain from action or threat . . . likely to worsen the situation" in Cyprus and called upon the communities and their leaders to act with the utmost restraint. It also recommended creation of a U.N. peace-keeping force. The secretary-general was requested, in agreement with Cyprus and the Guarantor Powers, to choose a mediator.[54] The United Nations force in Cyprus became operational in late March 1964. Thereafter any unilateral action or threat which was likely to worsen the situation in Cyprus would risk U.N. censure.

Since 1967 the United Nations force on Cyprus has maintained the peace, Makarios has strengthened his personal position, the Turkish Cypriots have consolidated their enclaves, and the Cypriot government has at once improved its overall situation and indicated that it is willing to meet a good number of the concerns of the Turkish Cypriots, while holding to its determination to legitimize its *de facto* revision of the 1960 constitution. Negotiation is going forward on such matters as re-definition of Turkish Cypriot rights, establishment of machinery to oversee enforcement of those rights, and the consequent re-entry of the Turkish minority into the national life of Cyprus. *Enosis,* despite its continued popularity among the Greek Cypriot masses, no longer is likely because of the opposition of President Makarios, AKEL, the Cypriot civil service, and the Greek Cypriot business community, all of whom have objections which converge with those of the Turkish Cypriots, Turkey, and the Soviet Union. Mass emigration of the Turkish Cypriots is unlikely because Ankara wants a continued Turkish presence on the island, and because most Turkish Cypriots want to stay anyway.

Although they want to improve their present situation, the Turkish Cypriots are still reluctant to weaken their defenses or bargaining position. Presently, however, the economic difficulties arising from high unemployment, overcrowding, and land shortage in the Turkish enclaves, which are viable only because of Turkish grants, make a settlement desirable from the standpoint of the Turkish Cypriots.

The Greek Cypriots, on the other hand, have enjoyed increasing prosperity. Nevertheless, a settlement would bring additional stability and normalization to all parts of Cyprus, and would therefore benefit the Greek as well as the Turkish Cypriot community.

---

[54] U.N. Document S/5575 (1964).

The withdrawal of most of the illegal Greek troops from Cyprus and the cooperation between the Greek and Turkish governments have reduced the dangers of an international conflict for the moment. Still, Greek and Turkish army officers remain in charge of antagonistic forces (the National Guard and the major Turkish enclaves), and negotiated revision of the Zurich-London arrangements is going slowly.

Recent history, as well as that of the more distant past, has shown that peaceful co-existence of the two Cypriot communities is unlikely without the presence on the island of a force sufficiently strong to dampen and depress outbreaks of inter-communal hostilities. For this reason, the presence of the United Nations force seems required at least until both Cypriot communities agree upon a settlement which they perceive to be truly just.[55]

On the other hand, the presence of United Nations forces has inhibited a settlement at the same time that it has controlled the fighting. While it has prevented a solution of the inter-communal conflict by force, it has not pressured either side into agreeing to a negotiated settlement. New patterns have developed while the fighting has been contained. Since the Cypriot government has managed to establish all the constitutional changes advocated by Makarios in December 1963, it may not feel that a formal settlement is desirable unless it legitimizes the gains of the Greek Cypriot leadership. To achieve a negotiated settlement acceptable to both Cypriot communities, carefully applied external pressure is probably necessary, but it must not be so forceful that either Greek or Turkish Cypriots sense a *diktat*. It was this feeling on the part of the Greek community that led to the destruction of the 1959-60 agreements.

Air Navigation

From time immemorial the Middle East has been the land bridge linking three continents: Europe, Asia and Africa. It also lies athwart some of the world's most significant bodies of water: the Black Sea, the Mediterranean, the Red Sea and the Persian Gulf—not to mention the Atlantic and the Indian Ocean beyond. But the Middle East is also of paramount importance from the standpoint of air navigation. In the words of one author, "air lanes stretching from all points between Copenhagen and Lisbon, to the West, and Tokyo and Australia, to the East, collect themselves at the hour-glass waist of the Arab states." [56] The strategic value of the area to the Great Powers for communication links accounts for its highly developed state of air transport in comparison to surface transport, even though the area itself is rather sparsely populated and not heavily developed from the economic standpoint. With the closure of the Suez Canal in 1967, access to air navigation has become of even greater significance than before, not only to the major trading nations, but to all the other countries which previously depended upon the canal for trade and commerce.

---

[55] Cyprus at present is the only country in the world with a United Nations peacekeeping force. See David H. Popper, "Lessons of United Nations Peacekeeping in Cyprus," *American Journal of International Law,* vol. 64, no. 4 (Sept. 1970), pp. 1-9.

[56] Keith Williams, "Commercial Aviation in Arab States: The Pattern of Control," *Middle East Journal,* vol. II, no. 2 (Spring, 1957), p. 138.

The United States has a significant interest in protection of air navigation rights through the Middle East.[57] In view of this country's involvement in Southeast Asia, suspension of air transit freedom in consequence of the June war of 1967 was cause for major concern. Europe and the Soviet Union are equally concerned. And for Israel, assured non-interference with its air communications is probably vital. Its only access to the rest of the world is by air and by sea, and the latter alone would be hardly sufficient in this era of rapid communications. The jets of Israel's El Al Airline—one could count them on one's fingers, almost on one hand—are essential to her international communications. In the circumstances, the consternation in Israel when one of these planes was hijacked to Algeria in 1968, and when two others were attacked by Arab guerrillas in Athens and Zurich in 1969, is hardly surprising. A few days after the Athens incident, on December 28, 1968, Israel launched a devastating retaliatory raid on Arab civil aircraft at Beirut International Airport, precipitating a political crisis in Lebanon.[58] On December 31, the United Nations Security Council condemned the Israeli act by unanimous vote. The incident brought about a total embargo by the French on arms supplies to Israel. The international consequences of the Beirut raid were underscored when it came to light that two of the three Arab airlines that lost a total of 13 commercial planes were owned or controlled largely by non-Arab interests, including several American companies and an American government agency, the Commodity Credit Corporation.[59]

The economic position of Lebanon, a country with no major heavy industry which exists primarily on its services and financial industries and (like Israel itself) is dependent on rapid air communication with Europe and the East, declined sharply. For a country of such great regional importance as Lebanon, in view of its traditional role in facilitating the political, commercial and diplomatic communications of the entire Arab world, questions of freedom of air navigation have become a matter of high priority in terms of national security, just as they have in Israel.

These incidents, not to mention the dramatic hijackings to Jordan and Egypt by Arab commandos in the summer of 1970, have demonstrated the urgency of providing some form of constructive international solution to the problem of violent attacks on commercial aviation.

The Law of International Air Navigation. Various theories have been advanced concerning the sovereignty of air space above states. Grotius, the classicist, seems to have considered that air space should be regarded as entirely free, like the high seas. Another theory, on the analogy to territorial waters, postulates a lower zone of territorial air space and a higher zone of free air space. Others have held that the air space above a state lies, to an unlimited extent, within the sovereignty of the subjacent state. Finally, it has been maintained that air space is within the

---

[57] For discussion see John S. Badeau, *The American Approach to the Arab World* (New York, 1968), pp. 21ff; George Lenczowski, ed., *United States Interests in the Middle East* (Washington, American Enterprise Institute, 2nd printing, 1968), p. 100.

[58] See Richard A. Falk, "The Beirut Raid and the International Law of Retaliation," *American Journal of International Law*, vol. 63, no. 3 (July, 1969), pp. 415-43.

[59] Details in *New York Times*, January 5, 1969. Also see Falk, "Beirut Raid."

sovereignty of the subjacent state but subject to a "servitude of innocent passage" for foreign civil but not military aircraft.[60] But these are just theories, not law. In contrast to the principles of international law relating to navigation by sea, which includes such well-settled concepts as "territorial waters" and the "high seas," there has not yet developed a body of customary international law embracing the right to fly, and this despite the fact that modern aircraft are capable of transporting passengers and goods to and from almost any place on earth more quickly than any other means.

What law there is tends to restrict rather than promote the free movement of aircraft, particularly in respect to flight over sovereign land areas. As one observer has noted, "There is no 'high air,' except over the high seas." [61] In the absence of settled customary law, international air navigation rights today are derived from a rather confusing array of international agreements or conventions, plus a large number of multi- or bilateral treaties. There are some eight international aviation conventions dealing with various aspects of the subject.[62] The general rules and principles of the Chicago Convention of 1944, which is probably the most important of these, are particularly significant as far as the Middle East is concerned. This convention has been adhered to by almost all the Middle Eastern states and by the Western powers, including the United States. Its basic provisions are also recognized by the Soviet Union. The convention was the product of a conference held in Chicago in 1944, attended by representatives from 52 nations, including Afghanistan, Egypt, Iran, Iraq, Lebanon, Syria and Turkey. The convention has since been ratified by most of the other Arab states and by Israel.

The Chicago Convention reaffirmed the principle, first set forth in the Paris Convention of 1919, that every state has complete and exclusive sovereignty over the airspace above its territory, including territorial waters. Most nations have come to subscribe to this principle and also to its counterpart: that outside a state's territorial airspace, in particular over the high seas, all have an equal right to fly. The convention also regulated to a considerable extent the right of the contracting parties to operate civil air flights, both scheduled and non-scheduled, in the airspace of one another. Nothing was agreed, however, about *state* aircraft (military, customs, police, diplomatic); such aircraft may not overfly or land in the territory of another state except with that state's permission. (Thus the U-2 flights disclosed in 1960 were, apart from any diplomatic ramifications, presumably illegal.) Scheduled *civil* air services flying over or landing within the territory of a contracting state are likewise subject to permission from the state in question. Scheduled flights which enter a state for the purpose of setting down passengers, mail or cargo are subject to terms prescribed by the state concerned, including any rules relating to prohibited areas and air traffic control. A case in point is that after the break in diplomatic relations between the United States and Syria during the June war of

---

[60] H. Lauterpacht, ed., *International Law*, by L. Oppenheim, 8th ed. (London, 1955), pp. 517-18; McNair, *The Law of the Air*, 2nd ed. (London, 1953), pp. 6-7.

[61] Williams, "Commercial Aviation in Arab States," p. 138.

[62] The eight conventions are Paris (1919), Havana (1928), Warsaw (1929), Rome (1933, two conventions), Chicago (1944), Geneva (1948), and Rome (1952). A useful compendium and reference is U.S. Senate, Committee on Commerce, *Air Laws and Treaties of the World*, vol. III (Washington, 1965), hereinafter cited as *Air Laws*.

1967, no scheduled American air service was allowed in Syria for more than two years. By contrast, however, permission for non-scheduled civil flights is not required provided the aircraft overflies the state without stopping, or stops only for such non-traffic purposes as to avoid bad weather, to refuel, or in the case of emergency.

In any case, however, whether the flight in question is scheduled or nonscheduled, the subjacent state reserves the right for reasons of military necessity or public safety to require all aircraft to fly prescribed routes over or into the state, and to require the aircraft to land. In December 1964 a private American plane operated by an oil company was shot down over the United Arab Republic for allegedly passing over prohibited areas and failing to heed Egyptian radio warnings.

The Chicago Convention also provided for the establishment of the International Civil Aviation Organization (ICAO). Administering the convention and operating subsequently as one of the specialized agencies of the United Nations, ICAO has played a central role in the development of recommended principles, standards and practices of international air navigation. Today there are more than a thousand aeronautical agreements registered with ICAO. Most of these are between states, but there are also many between states and airlines, as well as between airlines, or between airlines and other entities.[63]

Of even greater importance, perhaps, has been ICAO's function as a quasi-judicial body, to which international civil aviation disputes may be referred. It was before the ICAO, for instance, that the legal consequences of the Israeli raid on Beirut International Airport in December 1968 were subjected to the widest critical discussion and debate. ICAO provides a forum for consideration of revisions to existing conventions and the formulation of new ones. An example is the Tokyo Convention of 1963,[64] the first concerted international attempt to deal with illegal interference with, or seizure of, aircraft in flight, a subject considered in more detail below.

Air Agreements Affecting the Middle East. Most of the Middle Eastern countries, as members of the community of nations and as contracting parties to the Chicago Convention, are bound by the convention's general rules and principles. In addition, nearly all of them adhere to either one or the other of the so-called "Two Freedoms" or "Five Freedoms" agreements, also drawn up by the Chicago Conference of 1944. The "Two Freedoms" embodied in the International Air Service Transit Agreement require contracting states to grant to other contracting states:

1. the privilege for civil aircraft to fly across the other's territory in peacetime without landing, upon accepting the subjacent state's right to prohibit planes from flying over specified portions of its territory for reasons of military necessity or public safety; and

2. the privilege to land for non-traffic purposes such as refueling, emergencies and to avoid inclement weather.

---

[63] William W. Bishop, Jr., *International Law: Cases and Materials,* 2nd ed. (Boston, 1962), no. 65, p. 376. See also D. H. N. Johnson, *Rights in Air Space* (Manchester, 1965), pp. 58-59.

[64] Text in *American Journal of International Law,* vol. 58 (1964), p. 566.

The International Air Transport Agreement (the so-called "Five Freedoms" agreement) restated these two privileges and added three others:

> 3. the privilege for civil aircraft to put down passengers, mail and cargo taken on in the territory of the state whose nationality the aircraft possesses;
>
> 4. the privilege to take on passengers, mail and cargo destined for the territory of the state whose nationality the aircraft possesses; and
>
> 5. the right to take on and put down passengers, mail and cargo destined for the territory of any state.

While the first two freedoms involve privileges of flight in general, the third, fourth and fifth involve more specific rights related to trade and commerce. As noted in an article in *Foreign Affairs* in 1945 by Edward Warner, one of the American delegates to the Chicago conference, the five freedoms taken together would make it possible for an airline of a state signatory to the agreement to operate without any further special permission on any direct route from its homeland, picking up and dropping traffic en route at the civil airports of all other signatories. The "Five Freedoms" agreement, however, while originally signed by a score of states, including Lebanon, Turkey and Afghanistan, has enjoyed less success than the "Two Freedoms" agreement and a number of states, including the United States, have withdrawn from it in favor of the latter.

It may be noted that as part of the Arab League's political and economic boycott of Israel, the Arab states of the Middle East withhold all "Five Freedoms" from Israeli airlines. Moreover, the first freedom (i.e., the privilege of a licensed carrier of one carrier to transit the airspace of another country without stopping) is withheld from any aircraft attempting to transit Arab airspace directly after having departed from an Israeli airport. Among themselves, however, the Arab governments by and large freely exchange the first four freedoms, while generally withholding the fifth, for competitive commercial reasons.

Bilateral Agreements. Insofar as states do not adhere to the multilateral conventions, the right to fly over or to land in the territory of a Middle Eastern state must be obtained by means of a bilateral treaty. (Lebanon, however, still adheres to the "Five Freedoms" agreement.) The basic model for bilateral agreements entered into by the United States since 1944 has been the Chicago Conference's Resolution VIII, Standard Form of Agreement for Provisional Air Routes. According to Professor Bishop:

> These bilateral air transport agreements provide for exchange of air routes to be used by designated airlines of the respective countries; equality of treatment and nondiscrimination with respect to airport charges, customs duties, and inspection fees; reciprocal recognition of airworthiness certificates and personnel licenses; compliance with laws and regulations on entry, clearance, and procedure for amending the annex. The annex to the Chicago-type agreement usually describes the routes and traffic points granted to air service of each party, but imposes no restriction on capacity of aircraft or number of schedules and makes no provision for rate determination.[65]

---

[65] Bishop, *International Law.*

The United States had such bilateral agreements with Iran, Israel, Syria, Turkey and the UAR as of 1965.[66] Each of these granted to the United States air transport rights similar to those normally afforded other Western nations. Both Israel and Turkey require that all U.S. carriers using their airspace stop in their countries. Turkey's proximity to the Soviet Union probably accounts for its restrictiveness with regard to overflight rights; in both countries, however, officials seem to want to be in a position to account for all flights using their national airspace. In Iraq and Saudi Arabia, American carriers operate without air transport agreements.[67]

In normal times there are two main corridors open to the United States for overflying the Middle East. One involves flying over Lebanon, Syria, Iraq and Iran; the other over Egypt and Saudi Arabia. During past hostilities one or both of these corridors have been blocked; the importance of being able to keep them open is self-evident.

Skyjacking. In recent years the hijacking of civil aircraft has become a cause of acute concern.[68] According to the Federal Aviation Agency, 88 American planes (carriers and general aviation) were forcibly diverted from their scheduled destinations during the period 1961-71—79 of them to Cuba. Of the total of 88 hijackings, 33 occurred in 1969, 18 in 1970 and 12 in 1971. In addition, the International Air Transport Association (IATA), a private organization with a membership of more than 100 airlines, listed some 90 instances of hijacking during 1968 and the first eight months of 1969 alone. IATA has called for government action at the highest levels to mete out "very, very heavy punishment" to hijackers so as to deter others.

Hijacking was employed in the capture of former Congolese President Moise Tshombe when the plane on which he was a passenger was forced to fly to Algiers in 1967, where he was detained until his death in 1969.

As far as United States airlines are concerned, skyjacking remained essentially a Western Hemisphere problem until 1969, when a scheduled TWA jetliner was diverted from a Rome-Tel Aviv route and forced by two members of the Palestinian Liberation Front to fly to Damascus. While the motives of Cuban hijackers generally appear to be unrelated to any guerrilla activity against the United States, the motives of Arab hijackers are overtly political. Palestinian sources advanced several goals expected to be achieved in the 1969 Damascus incident: one of the passengers, "an Israeli responsible for the death and misery of numerous Palestinians," was to be captured and tried by a revolutionary court; aggressive actions should be undertaken against the United States as an "imperialist supporter of Israel"; and some of the Israeli citizens on board would be held as hostages for the exchange of Arab prisoners in Israel. In the diplomatic maneuvering that ensued, the U.S. government labeled the incident as a criminal act of international piracy, and accused Syria of condoning the act by detaining the six Israeli passengers on board. Israel held both the Syrian and American governments responsible for the safety and release of all the passengers regardless of nationality.

---

[66] Committee on Commerce, *Air Laws,* vol. III, pp. 4410-18.

[67] Ibid., p. 440.

[68] See, generally, Alona E. Evans, "Aircraft Hijacking: Its Cause and Cure," *American Journal of International Law,* vol. 63, no. 4 (October 1969), pp. 695-710.

The United States has taken the initiative in pushing for stronger international agreements to deter and punish hijackers. It recognizes that the opportunities for guerrilla groups to dramatize their grievances in this way have tremendous implications for political and commercial interests in a world dependent on air travel, to say nothing of the concern of the individual for his own safety. The U.S. ratified the Tokyo Convention, referred to above, in September 1969. The convention came into force on December 4, 1969, following ratification by twelve of the signatory states.[69] It deals with crimes committed aboard a plane in flight, such as skyjacking, and calls for the immediate return of such a plane, together with its crew and passengers. Before the ink was dry there were clamors for stronger controls. The 44,000-member International Federation of Airline Pilots Association (IFALPA) pointed out that the Tokyo Convention failed to cover (1) crimes committed against an aircraft while the plane is on the ground, such as the incidents at Athens, Zurich and Munich; and (2) punishment of the skyjacker upon his being apprehended—a measure sidestepped by the Syrians in the case of the TWA jet diverted to Damascus. IFALPA appealed through diplomatic channels to various bodies, including the United Nations Security Council, for more severe sanctions. IATA has also been exceedingly active in pressing for stronger legislation, both domestic and international. As the result of these and other pressures, a new Convention for the Suppression of Unlawful Seizure of Aircraft was signed at The Hague on December 16, 1970. Within a month it had attracted 51 signatories, a powerful indication of the widely felt need for stronger controls.[70] Its provisions, which are essentially supplementary to those of the Tokyo Convention, call for punishment by "severe penalties" of any person who unlawfully seizes or exercises control of an aircraft in flight, or attempts to do so, or is an accomplice of such a person. Conclusion of the convention, which had languished through several drafts over a period of years, was unquestionably hastened by the Middle East incidents of 1969 and 1970.

Following the September 1970 hijackings of four aircraft which were brought to and destroyed in Jordan, the incidence of this kind of violence in the Middle East decreased. As far as the countries most directly involved are concerned, it would seem to be in the interests of both the Arabs and the Israelis that the civil aviation of neither is forced out of the air.

---

[69] Ibid., p. 707.

[70] Text in *International Legal Materials,* vol. X, no. 1 (January 1971), pp. 133-36. The Convention comes into force when ratified by ten of the original signatory powers. For background, see Evans, p. 708.

VI. CONCLUSION

The material in the preceding chapters provides the basis for a number of observations that can be made about the relationship of international law to the Middle East.

First of all, it is worth noting the extent to which the countries of the Middle East—and in particular the successor states to the Ottoman Empire—have adapted themselves to the predominantly Western legal concepts and procedures of modern international law insofar as their external relations are concerned. It is difficult for any Westerner to appreciate just how great an adjustment this has been for most of these countries and societies, particularly in the light of the inherent conservatism of Islamic law, and of other aspects of their culture as well. For the most part, the impact of the West has been met with considerable resistance and often with resentment or hostility. By contrast, accepted standards of international law have taken hold to a surprising extent.

Equally significant is the extent to which Middle Eastern governments have participated in organizations, treaties and conventions regulating many forms of peaceful conduct among men and nations. Aside from the United Nations itself, one could cite many examples: the International Telecommunications Union, the Universal Postal Union, the International Civil Aviation Organization, the International Monetary Fund, and the International Bank for Reconstruction and Development (World Bank) and its related agencies. Most of these arrangements have escaped attention in this book precisely because they are so well established that they give rise to little controversy, at least as far as the Middle East is concerned. One tends to take it for granted that the mail will go through; that diplomats have immunity; that passports will be honored; that a traveler in trouble may properly invoke the assistance of his country's consul; that a check cashed in Beirut will be honored in New York; that highway signs in Iran have the same significance that they have in France and in most of the countries in between. It is worth pausing to reflect that the smooth development of international affairs on day-to-day matters of this kind goes hand in hand with an accepted and codified body of international law. This is the undramatic result of the slow and often painstaking evolution of internationally accepted norms of conduct which are grounded ultimately in what we call "law." In this development the countries of the Middle East have, for the most part, extended their full share of cooperation.

Where the application of the standards of international law rubs up against important and conflicting national interests, as so often appears to be the case in the Middle East, matters cannot always be resolved in so routine and unobtrusive a fashion. The most conspicuous example of this, of course, is the struggle over Palestine. Even here, however, one can see that most of the problems are susceptible to objective legal analysis, even if they are not necessarily amenable to immediate solution by juridical means. It would be helpful and constructive if policy makers were to perceive more clearly that this is the case, for in the widespread quest for a peaceful solution to the Palestine question international law has unfortunately played a role secondary to political debate, nationalistic and historical divisiveness, and the resort to force. It seems possible that, if given a chance, law may eventually make a contribution parallel to that of other disciplines. After all, one attribute of the law is its coolness; its coinage is in reason rather than emotion, calmness rather than excitement. This applies even in the case of what is known as the "Law of War." Its evolution has been tortuous, but progress has been made—not only in the rules of warfare itself, but in emphasizing the inadmissibility of unrestrained military activity as far as civilians are concerned. In this area the law admittedly lags behind the battlefield. It took World War I to produce the Kellogg-Briand Pact, and it took World War II to produce the Geneva Conventions of 1949. The nuclear nonproliferation treaty ensued from the Cold War, and whatever ultimately emerges relating to germ warfare will have been spurred on by the war in Southeast Asia. By the same token, it seems possible that one outcome of the conflict in the Middle East will be acceptance of some code of legally enforceable principles whereby the inhabitants of territory coveted by rival nationalities can co-exist without the threat of recurrent bloodshed.

In this connection it would be well to bear in mind the position of the United Nations. After all, the U.N. General Assembly is one of the few places in the world where official representatives of the governments of Israel and its Arab antagonists are able to be seated peaceably together. The United Nations provides no panacea, and idealists sometimes do it a disservice by oversimplifying its powers and responsibilities. The U.N. is not always effective in preventing the outbreak of hostilities, it is chronically in financial straits, and all too often it takes on the aspect of a vast echo chamber ringing with righteous nationalism. But to view the United Nations so negatively is to dismiss too lightly its achievements and the potential role it can still play. Even in the most adverse circumstances, as in Cyprus, it has performed valuable peace-keeping services. It has also provided a reasonably effective channel for humanitarian relief and assistance, as in the case of UNRWA.

Most important, the United Nations provides a forum where political and diplomatic negotiations can be conducted seriously, professionally, and with discretion. The unanimous Security Council Resolution 242 of November 22, 1967, is perhaps the most significant Security Council resolution ever passed insofar as the Middle East is concerned. It was hammered out by experts after arduous negotiation; almost every word has its own import. It is general in its structure, yet remarkably clear and precise in its mandate. It not only provides a succinct summary of every major problem that must be solved, but also offers a means whereby a solution may ultimately be reached. Perhaps it is not perfect, any more than Woodrow Wilson's Fourteen Points were perfect, but it does provide a reference point of rationality and common sense that can be turned to when matters threaten to get out of balance. Except to extremists on either side, it provides a framework that should be acceptable to all the parties involved, and it has the active support of the major powers. Moreover, it is a legal as well as a political document, in that it provides a basis for application of well-established legal principles to the solution of problems which in the absence of Resolution 242 might well prove to be insuperable.

International law is in a constant state of evolution. No one would deny that it has its inadequacies. But perhaps out of the Middle East turmoil, paradoxical as it may seem, will come new standards of international law which in due course will provide a useful guide and example for seekers after peace throughout the world.

INDEX

Turkey, 1-4, 8, 16, 32, 101, 116, 117, 119, 120, 128, 131; and the Baghdad Pact (later CENTO), 9, 10; and the Turkish Straits, 65-71; and Cyprus, 121-126; and the Turko-Iraqi Treaty, 118. *See also* Ottoman Empire

Turko-Iraqi Pact. *See* Turkey

United Arab Republic. *See* Egypt

United Nations, 5, 6, 9, 12, 14, 16, 17, 21, 23, 28, 30-32, 34-36, 38, 41, 44, 49, 51-53, 55, 60, 62, 71, 74, 75, 81, 104, 107, 110; and Security Council Resolution No. 242, 17-20, 27, 29, 30-32, 50, 62, 72, 77, 81, 109, 134, 135; and Palestinian Conciliation Commission, 129, 133; and the International Aviation Organization, 129, 183; and the Human Rights Commission, 49; and UNEF, 52, 78, 85 (*see also* Egypt); and Cyprus, 122, 125, 126

United Nations Charter, 22, 24-28, 30, 31, 35, 72, 77

United Nations Relief and Works Agency, 55, 57-59, 61, 62, 110. *See also* Palestinian refugees

United States, 28, 29, 33, 38, 55, 58, 60, 111, 127, 128, 131, 132; and the Turkish Straits, 69, 71; and the Supreme Court, 43, 109; and Cyprus, 121

U.S.S.R. *See* **Russia**

U Thant (secretary general of the U.N.), 61

West Bank, 39, 40, 50, 51, 108; Israeli occupation, 37, 42, 44, 46; and the Palestinian refugees, 61

World Zionist Organization, 13

World War II, 8-10, 30, 43

Yemen, 4, 86, 87

Yemen, Republic of, 86, 87

Yemen, South, 86

Zionism, 13, 35